American Mathematics Competitions (AMC 8)
Preparation

Volume 1

http://www.mymathcounts.com/index.php

The American Mathematics Competitions 8 is a 25-question multiple-choice contest for students in the sixth through eighth grade. Accelerated fourth and fifth graders can also take part. The AMC 8 is administered in schools in November. The American Mathematics Competitions (AMC) publishes the Achievement Roll list recognizing students in 6th grade and below who scored 15 or above, and the Honor Roll list recognizing students who score in the top 5%, and the Distinguished Honor Roll list recognizing students who score in the top 1%.

This book can be used by 5th to 8th grade students preparing for AMC 8. Each chapter consists of (1) basic skill and knowledge section with plenty of examples, (2) about 30 exercise problems, and (3) detailed solutions to all problems.

We would like to thank the American Mathematics Competitions (AMC 8 and 10) for their mathematical ideas. Many problems (marked by ☆) in this book are inspired from these tests. We only cited very few problems directly from these tests for the purpose of comparison with our own solutions.

We would also like to thank the following students who kindly reviewed the manuscripts and made valuable suggestions and corrections: Albert Hao, Sean Jung, Sameer Khan, Aadith Menon, Jeffery Shen, William Sun, Joy Shi, Yang Wei, and Samuel Yoon.

ISBN-13: 978-1500614195
ISBN-10: 150061419X

Please contact mymathcounts@gmail.com for suggestions, corrections, or clarifications.

Table of Contents

This page is intentionally left blank.

1. BASIC KNOWLEDGE

Abbreviations:

Perimeter = P Area = A or S Length = l Width = w

Height = h Circumference = C Radius = r

Side lengths of a polygon = $a,\ b,\ c,\ ...$

Basic Formulas for Perimeters and Areas

Triangle:

Perimeter of a triangle: $P = a + b + c$

Area of a triangle: $A = \dfrac{1}{2}bh_b$, h_b is the height on the side b.

For an equilateral triangle (three sides have the same length, a), the area is

$A = \dfrac{1}{4}a^2\sqrt{3}$.

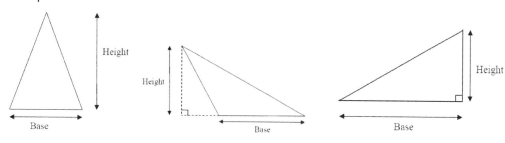

Heron Formula Area of a triangle with sides a, b, and c:

$$A = \sqrt{s(s-a)(s-b)(s-c)}, \text{ where } s = \frac{1}{2}(a+b+c) \text{ and } a,\ b, \text{ and } c \text{ are the three}$$

sides.

Example 1. The area of triangle ABC is 16 cm^2. D and E are midpoints of AB and AC, respectively. F is a point on BC such that $BF = 3$ cm. What is the area of triangle DEF ?

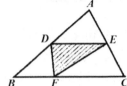

(A) 12   (B) 9   (C) 8   (D) 4   (E) 3

Solution: D.
Let G be the midpoint of BC. Connect GD and GE.
Then $\Delta DEG \sim \Delta ABC$.

Therefore $S_{\Delta DEG} = \dfrac{1}{4} S_{\Delta ABC}$.

Since $DE // BC$, $S_{\Delta DEF} = S_{\Delta DEG}$.

Therefore the shaded area $= \dfrac{1}{4} S_{\Delta ABC} = 4$ cm^2.

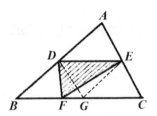

Note that F can be any point on BC.

Example 2. What is the area of a right triangle whose legs measure 10 cm and 18 cm respectively?
(A) 180 cm^2 (B) 100 cm^2 (C) 90 cm^2 (D) 60 cm^2 (E) 30 cm^2

Solution: C.
Since the triangle is a right triangle, any of the two legs can be the height and the other leg will be the base.

$$A = \frac{1}{2} bh_b = \frac{1}{2} \times 10 \times 18 = 90.$$

Example 3. If $BD = DC$ and the area of the triangle ABD is 8 cm^2, find the area of triangle ABC.
(A) 16 cm^2 (B) 8 cm^2 (C) 14 cm^2 (D) 32 cm^2 (E) 4 cm^2

Solution: A.

Since triangles ABD and ADC have the same height and the same base, their areas are the same. $A_{\triangle ABC} = A_{\triangle ABD} + A_{\triangle ADC} = 8 + 8 = 16$.

Example 4. The area of a triangle is 24 square units, and its base is 6 units. How many units are in the length of the height ?
(A) 24   (B) 12   (C) 10   (D) 8   (E) 6

Solution: D.

$$A = \frac{1}{2}bh_b$$

$$24 = \frac{1}{2} \times 6 \times h_b \qquad \Rightarrow \qquad h_b = 8.$$

Example 5. Find the area of the triangle with the side lengths of 21, 28, and 35.
(A) 84   (B) 42   (C) 144   (D) 288   (E) 294

Solution: E.

Method 1:

Perimeter = 21 + 28 + 35 = 84. $s = \dfrac{84}{2} = 42$

$$A = \sqrt{s(s-a)(s-b)(s-c)} = \sqrt{42(42-21)(42-28)(42-35)} = 294$$

Method 2:

The triangle is a right triangle with two legs of 21 and 28. The area is

$$A = \frac{1}{2}b \times h = \frac{1}{2} \times 21 \times 28 = 294 .$$

Rectangle and Parallelogram:

Perimeter: $P = 2(L + W)$ Area: $A = L \times W$

This can be thought as the area of two triangles added together.

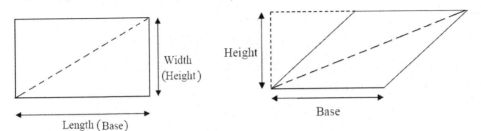

In the parallelogram $ABCD$, T is any interior point, we have always:

$$S_{\triangle TAB} + S_{\triangle TCD} = \frac{1}{2} \times S_{ABCD}$$

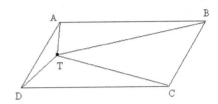

Area of A Rectangle with Four Cut Areas

The rectangle is divided into four rectangles with areas as shown.

a	b
d	c

The following relationship is true: $a \times c = b \times d$

☆**Example 6.** (AMC 12) A large rectangle is partitioned into four rectangles by two segments parallel to its sides. The areas of three of the resulting rectangles are shown. What is the area of the fourth rectangle?

6	14
x	35

(A) 10   (B) 15   (C) 20   (D) 21   (E) 25

Solution: B.
Method 1 (our solution):
$6 \times 35 = 14 \times x$ $\Rightarrow$ $x = 15$.

Method 2 (official solution)

Rectangles of the same height have areas proportional to their

bases, a and b. Hence $\dfrac{6}{14} = \dfrac{a}{b} = \dfrac{?}{35}$, so the required area is 15.

a b

Method 3 (official solution)
We can prove that the product of the areas of the diagonally
opposite rectangles is the same: If segment lengths are x, y,
u and v as shown, then the product of the areas of the lower
left and upper right is $(xv)(yu)$ and the product of the other
areas is $(xu)(yv)$. Since $(35)(6) = (14)(?)$, the area of the
fourth rectangle is $(35)(6)/14 = 15$.

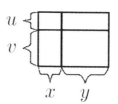

u
v

x y

Method 4 (official solution)
For the given data, we can find the answer by factoring the
areas. Since rectangles of the same height have areas
proportional to their bases, the unknown area is $r{\cdot}s = 3{\cdot}5 = 15$.
This factoring method will not work for all given data; e.g., if
16 is substituted for 14.

3·2	7·2
$r{\cdot}s$	7·5

The Pick's Law (Finding the area of the region bounded by grids)

For unit rectangular grid: $Area = \dfrac{B}{2} + I - 1$

For unit triangular grid: $Area = B + 2I - 2$

B: Number of boundary points. I: Number of interior point.

☆**Example 7.** (AMC 8) The horizontal and vertical distances between adjacent
points equal 1 unit. The area of triangle ABC is
(A) 1/4   (B) 1/2   (C) 3/4   (D) 1   (E) 5/4

Solution: B.
Method 1 (official solution):
$$S_{\triangle ABC} = S_{\triangle ADC} - S_{\triangle ABF} - 2S_{\triangle FDB} - S_{\triangle BCE}$$

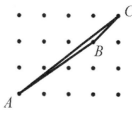

$$= \frac{1}{2} \times 4 \times 3 - \frac{1}{2} \times 3 \times 2 - 2 \times \frac{1}{2} \times 1 \times 2 - \frac{1}{2} \times 1 \times 1 = \frac{1}{2}$$

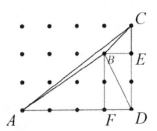

Method 2 (our solution):

By **Pick's Law**, $Area = \frac{3}{2} + 0 - 1 = \frac{1}{2}$.

☆**Example 8.** What is the area enclosed by the geoboard quadrilateral below?
(A) 16   (B) 18   (C) 20   (D) 25   (E) 21

Solution: D.

$B = 6, I = 23.$

By Pick's Theorem, $Area = \frac{B}{2} + I - 1 =$

$Area = \frac{6}{2} + 23 - 1 = 25.$

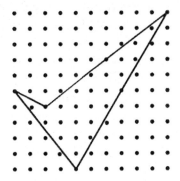

Example 9. A rectangle is cut from the corner of a larger rectangle as shown. How many feet are in the perimeter of the shape?
(A) 24   (B) 22   (C) 20   (D) 18   (E) 10

Solution: B.
A good way to solve this problem is to move two red colored sides to each end. (Note the perimeter does not change before and after moving). After doing that, a rectangle is formed with known side lengths. The perimeter is $P = 2(L + W) = 2(6 + 5) = 22'$.

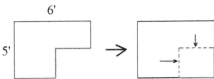

☆**Example 10.** (AMC 8) The area of polygon $ABCDEF$ is 52 with $AB = 8$, $BC =$ 9 and $FA = 5$. What is $DE + EF$?

(A) 7   (B) 8   (C) 9   (D) 10   (E) 11

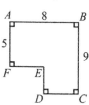

Solution: C.

Method 1 (official solution):

Rectangle $ABCG$ has area $8 \times 9 = 72$, so rectangle $FEDG$ has area $72 - 52 = 20$.

The length of FG equals $DE = 9 - 5 = 4$, so the length of EF is $20/4 = 5$.

Therefore, $DE + EF = 4 + 5 = 9$.

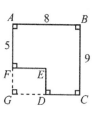

Method 2 (our solution):

Extend FE to meet BC at G. $ED = 9 - 5 = 4$.

$EG = 8 - x$.

Rectangle $ABFG$ has area $5 \times 8 = 40$, so rectangle $FGDG$ has area $52 - 40 = 12$.

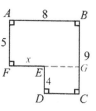

So $(8 - x) \times 4 = 12 \quad \Rightarrow \quad x = 5$.

Therefore, $DE + EF = 4 + 5 = 9$.

Example 11. What is the minimum number of 1cm square tiles that would cover this figure?

(A) 48   (B) 22   (C) 36   (D) 100   (E) 60

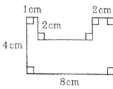

Solution: B.

$a + b + c = 4 \times 1 + 5 \times 2 + 4 \times 2 = 4 + 10 + 8 = 22$ cm^2.

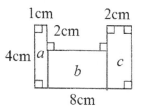

Example 12. *ABCD* is a 4 × 6 rectangle formed by three 4 × 2 small rectangles. *B* and *E* are the centers of the arcs *AG* and *FC*, respectively. Find the shaded area.

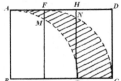

(A) 6   (B) 9   (C) 8   (D) 10   (E) 12

Solution: C.

The shaded area is the same as the area of the rectangle *FHGE*, which is 4 × 2 = 8.

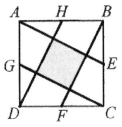

Example 13. Square *ABCD* has midpoints *E, F, G,* and *H*. *AB* = 15 centimeters. Find the area of the shaded interior square in square centimeters.

(A) 46   (B) 49   (C) 45   (D) 56   (E) 55

Solution: C.

The shaded area is $\dfrac{1}{5}S_{ABCD} = \dfrac{1}{5} \times 15 \times 15 = 45$.

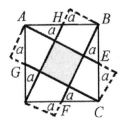
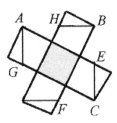

Trapezoid:

Area of a Trapezoid: $A = \dfrac{(b_1 + b_2)}{2}h$

This can be thought as the area of two triangles added together

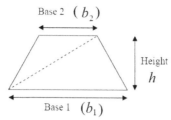

Example 14. What is the number of square centimeters in the area of the trapezoid shown?

(A) 36   (B) 38   (C) 40   (D) 48   (E) 56

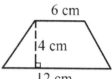

Solution: A.

Area of a Trapezoid:

$$A = \frac{(b_1 + b_2)}{2} h = \frac{(6+12)}{2} \times 4 = 9 \times 4 = 36.$$

☆**Example 15.** (AMC 8) In trapezoid $ABCD$, AD is perpendicular to DC, $AD = AB = 3$, and $DC = 6$. In addition, E is on DC, and BE is parallel to AD. Find the area of $\triangle BEC$.

(A) 3   (B) 4.5   (C) 6   (D) 9   (E) 18

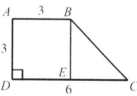

Solution: B.

Method 1 (official solution)

The area of the $4BEC$ is the area of the trapezoid $ABCD$ minus the area of the square $ABED$. The area of $\triangle BEC$ is

$$A = \frac{(3+6)}{2} \times 3 - 3^2 = 13.5 - 9 = 4.5.$$

Method 2 (our solution):

$\triangle BEC$ is an isosceles right triangle with two legs both

measuring 3. So the area is $A = \dfrac{3 \times 3}{2} = 4.5.$

Example 16. Find the area of the shaded region within the trapezoid if $AB = 12$, $BC = 8$, $CD = 10$, and $\overline{AB}$ is perpendicular to $\overline{BC}$.

(A) 88   (B) 40   (C) 60   (D) 44   (E) 20

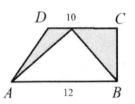

Solution: B.

Method 1:

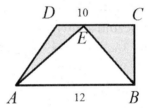

The area of the trapezoid is $A = \dfrac{(10+12)}{2} \times 8 = 88$.

The area of the shaded region

$$S_{ABCD} - S_{\triangle ABE} = 88 - \frac{1}{2} \times 12 \times 8 = 40 \ (\text{units}^2).$$

Method 2:

$$S_{\triangle AED} + S_{ABEC} = \frac{1}{2} \times DE \times BC + \frac{1}{2} \times EC \times BC$$

$$= \frac{1}{2} \times BC \times (DE + EC) = \frac{1}{2} \times 8 \times 10 = 40 \ (\text{units}^2).$$

Rhombus:

Perimeter of a rhombus: $P = 4a$ (a is the side length).

Area of a rhombus: $A = \dfrac{1}{2} d_1 \times d_2$ (d_1 and d_2 are diagonals).

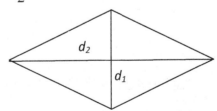

☆**Example 17.** (AMC 8) Points A, B, C and D are midpoints of the sides of the larger square. If the larger square has area 60, what is the area of the smaller square?

(A) 15   (B) 20   (C) 24   (D) 30   (E) 40

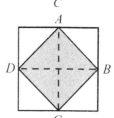

Solution: (D).

Method 1 (official solution):
Divide the larger square into 8 congruent triangles, as shown, 4 of which make up the smaller square. The area of the smaller square is 4/8 or 1/2 of the area of the larger square, so the area of the smaller square is equal to 30.

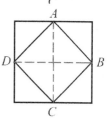

Method 2 (our solution):
Connect AC and DB. $ABCD$ is a rhombus.

The area $A = \dfrac{1}{2}d_1 \times d_2 = \dfrac{1}{2} \times AC \times DB = \dfrac{1}{2} \times 60 = 30$.

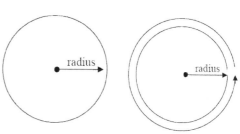

Circle:

Circumference (perimeter) $C = 2\pi r$

Area of a circle: $A = \pi r^2 = \dfrac{\pi}{4}d^2$

d is the diameter of the circle. $d = 2r$

Sector:

Given a sector of a circle where l is the length of the arc and A is the area of the sector:

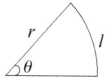

$$l = 2\pi r \times \dfrac{\theta}{360}. \qquad A = \pi r^2 \times \dfrac{\theta}{360}.$$

Example 18. What is the area of a circle whose radius measures 4 cm?

(A) 16π (B) 18π (C) 20π (D) 64π (E) 49π

Solution: A.

$A = \pi r^2 = \pi \times 4^2 = 16\pi$ cm^2.

Example 19. What is the radius of a circle whose area is 64π cm^2?

(A) 64   (B) 32   (C) 16   (D) 8   (E) 128

Solution: D.

$A = \pi r^2 = 64\pi$ $\Rightarrow$ $64\pi = \pi \times r^2$ $\Rightarrow$ $64 = r^2$ $\Rightarrow$ $r = 8$.

Example 20. Find in terms of π the number of square inches in the area of the shaded region formed by the intersecting diameters of a circle with radius 6.

(A) 16π (B) 12π (C) 20π (D) 64π (E) 36π

Solution: B.

The sum of the angles of the shaded sectors is 120°. The shaded area is:

$A = \pi r^2 \times \dfrac{\theta}{360} = \pi \times 6^2 \times \dfrac{120}{360} = 36\pi \times \dfrac{1}{3} = 12\pi$.

☆**Example 21.** Four circles of radius 3 are drawn with the centers at the vertices of a square. The regions inside the square are shown. Find the area of the shaded region.

(A) $36 - 24\pi$ (B) $36 - 12\pi$

(C) $36 - 9\pi$ (D) $81 - 12\pi$

(E) $81 - 9\pi$

Solution: C.

The four quarter-circles that lie inside the square have a total area equal to the area of one of the circles, 9π. The area of the square is $(3 + 3)(3 + 3) = 36$.
The answer is $36 - 9\pi$.

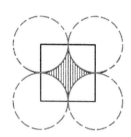

☆**Example 22.** (AMC 10) Circles A, B, and C each have radius 1. Circles A and B share one point of tangency. Circle C has a point of tangency with the midpoint of AB. What is the area inside circle C but outside circle A and circle B ?

(A) $3 - \dfrac{\pi}{2}$ (B) $\dfrac{\pi}{2}$ (C) 2 (D) $\dfrac{3\pi}{4}$ (E) $1 + \dfrac{\pi}{2}$

Solution: C.
Method 1 (official solution)
Let D be the midpoint of AB, and let circle C intersect circles A and B at E and F, respectively, distinct from D. The shaded portion of unit

square $ADCE$ has area $1 - \dfrac{\pi}{4}$, as does the shaded portion

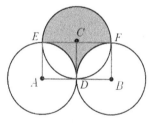

of unit square $BDCF$. The portion of the shaded region which is outside these squares is a semicircle of radius 1

and has area $\dfrac{\pi}{2}$. The total shaded area is $2(1 - \dfrac{\pi}{4}) + \dfrac{\pi}{2}$

$= 2$.

Method 2 (official solution)
Let D be the midpoint of AB, and let circle C intersect circles A and B at E and F, respectively, distinct from D. Let G be diametrically opposite D on circle C. The shaded area to the area of square $DFGE$, which has diagonal length 2. Its side length is $\sqrt{2}$ and its area is 2.

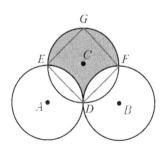

Method 3 (our solution)

The shaded area = the area of circle $C - 2x$

We only need to find x.

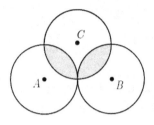 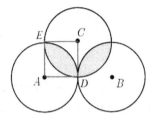 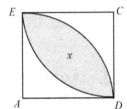

$$y = S_{ADCE} - S_{\text{Sector } ADE} = S_{\text{Sector } CDE} = 1 - \frac{\pi \times 1^2}{4} = 1 - \frac{\pi}{4}$$

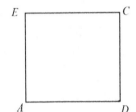 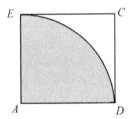 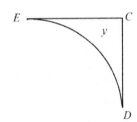

$$x = S_{ADCE} - 2y = 1 - 2(1 - \frac{\pi}{4}) = \frac{\pi}{2} - 1$$

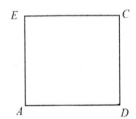 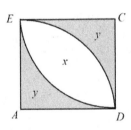 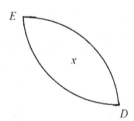

The answer is $\pi \times 1^2 - 2(\frac{\pi}{2} - 1) = 2$.

Example 23. *ABCD* is a square with vertex *A* at the center of the circle. *AE* = 10 in. What is the number of square inches in the area of △*BCD*?

(A) 100   (B) 50   (C) 25   (D) 8π   (E) 12π

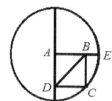

Solution: C.

Connect AC. We see that *AC, DB,* and *AE* are all radius of the circle. So *AC = DB = AE* = 10.

Thus $S_{\triangle BCD} = \dfrac{1}{2} \times S_{ABCD} = \dfrac{1}{2} \times \dfrac{10 \times 10}{2} = 25$.

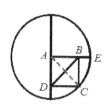

Example 24. The length of a side of equilateral triangle *ABC* is 12. *D, E,* and *F* are the midpoints of $\overline{AB}$, $\overline{BC}$, and $\overline{AC}$, respectively. *A, B,* and *C* are the centers of the circles that contain arcs *DF, DE,* and *FE,* respectively. What is the area of the shaded region?

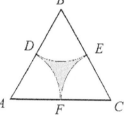

(A) $72\sqrt{3} - 18\pi$ (B) $36\sqrt{3} - 9\pi$

(C) $72\sqrt{3} - 9\pi$ (D) $36\sqrt{2} - 18\pi$

(E) $36\sqrt{3} - 18\pi$

Solution: E.

Shaded area = the area of triangle *ABC* − (the area of sector *ADF* + the area of sector *CEF* + the area of sector *BDE*)

= the area of triangle *ABC* − 3 × (the area of sector *ADF*) =

$\dfrac{\sqrt{3}}{4} \times 12^2 - 3 \times (\dfrac{60}{360} \times \pi \times AD^2) = 36\sqrt{3} - 3 \times (\dfrac{60}{360} \times \pi \times 6^2) = 36\sqrt{3} - 18\pi$.

Example 25. In the rectangle shown, the radius of each quarter circle is 6. What is the area of the shaded region?

(A) $120 - 36\pi$

(B) 36π

(C) $200 - 36\pi$

(D) $120 - 18\pi$

(E) $240 - 36\pi$

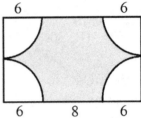

Solution: E.

Shaded area = the area of rectangle $ABCD$ − 4 × (the area of sector DEF)

$= 20 \times 12 - 4 \times (\frac{1}{4} \times \pi \times DF^2) = 240 - 36\pi$.

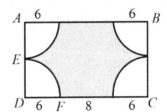

Example 26. In square $ABCD$, $AB = 1$. BD and AC are arcs of radius 1. Two shaded areas are the same. Find the difference of the unshaded areas.

(A) $\frac{\pi}{2} - 1$.   (B) $1 - \frac{\pi}{4}$.   (C) $\frac{\pi}{3} - 1$.

(D) $1 - \frac{\pi}{6}$.   (E) $2 - \frac{\pi}{2}$.

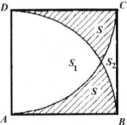

Solution: A.

The areas of S_1 and S form a quarter circle:

$$S_1 + S = \frac{\pi}{4} \quad \Rightarrow \quad S_1 = \frac{\pi}{4} - S$$

The areas of S_2 and S is obtained by subtracting the quarter circle from the square:

$$S_2 + S = 1 - \frac{\pi}{4} \quad \Rightarrow \quad S_2 = 1 - S - \frac{\pi}{4}.$$

Therefore, the difference of the unshaded areas is:

$$S_1 - S_2 = (\frac{\pi}{4} - S) - (1 - S - \frac{\pi}{4}) = \frac{\pi}{2} - 1.$$

Example 27. *D* and *C* trisect the arc of the half circle as shown in the figure. Find the shaded area if the area of the half circle is 9π.

(A) 3π (B) 4π (C) 5π (D) 6π (E) 2π

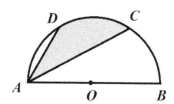

Solution: A.
Connect *OD* and *OC*.
Since $\overset{\frown}{AD} = \overset{\frown}{DC} = \overset{\frown}{CB}$, *CD//AB*.
$S_{\triangle OCD} = S_{\triangle ACD}$.
Therefore the shaded area is 1/3 of the area of the half circle: $9\pi/3 = 3\pi$.

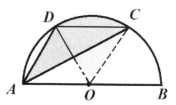

☆**Example 28.** Semi-circles of radius 2 and 3 are externally tangent and are circumscribed by a third semi-circle, as shown in the figure. Find the area of the shaded region.

(A) 3π (B) 4π (C) 6π (D) 9π (E) 12π

Solution: (C).
We draw a new figure as shown. The diameter of the large circle is $6 + 4 = 10$, so its radius is 5. Hence, the area of the shaded region in the new figure is $\pi(5^2) - (3^2) - \pi(2^2) = \pi(25 - 9 - 4) = 12\pi$.

The answer to the original problem is then $12\pi / 2 = 6\pi$.

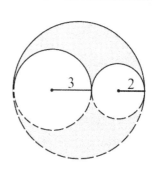

PROBLEMS

Problem 1. In the rectangle shown, the ratio of width to length is 1: 4. What percent of the rectangle is shaded?

(A) 80   (B) 20   (C) 50   (D) 44   (E) 30

Problem 2. If the area of rectangle $ABCD$ is 24, find the area of $\triangle ABD$.

(A) 20   (B) 12   (C) 10   (D) 8   (E) 6

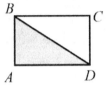

Problem 3. In rectangle $ACDE$, B lies on $\overline{AC}$, $DC = 4$ cm, and $DE = 8$ cm. Find the area of the shaded region.

(A) 16 cm^2 (B) 32 cm^2 (C) 64 cm^2 (D) 8 cm^2
(E) 10 cm^2

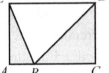

Problem 4. If the perimeter of an equilateral triangle is 60, what is the area of the triangle?

(A) $200\sqrt{3}$ (B) $100\sqrt{3}$ (C) 300   (D) 400   (E) $50\sqrt{3}$

Problem 5. The sides of a triangle are 5, 12, and 13. What is the number of square units in the area of the triangle?

(A) 78   (B) 30   (C) 121   (D) 156   (E) 312

Problem 6. What is the number of square centimeters in the area of a triangle whose sides measure 8 cm, 15 cm, and 17 cm?

(A) 120   (B) 60   (C) 255   (D) 68   (E) 34

Problem 7. In the figure shown, the lengths and widths of rectangles A, B, C, and D are whole numbers. The areas of rectangles A, B, and C are 35, 45, and 36, respectively. What is the area of the entire figure?

(A) 144   (B) 121   (C) 100   (D) 162   (E) 28

☆**Problem 8.** (AMC 8) Dots are spaced one unit apart, horizontally and vertically. The number of square units enclosed by the polygon is

(A) 5   (B) 6   (C) 7   (D) 8   (E) 9

Problem 9. How many inches are in the perimeter of the following figure? All angles shown are right angles.

(A) 38   (B) 32   (C)3   (D) 48   (E) 24

Problem 10. How many square feet are there in the house with the dimensions shown in the figure?

(A) 1468   (B) 1600   (C) 900   (D) 1000   (E) 1100

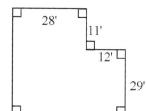

Problem 11. The perimeter of a rectangle is 46. The difference between the length and the width of the rectangle is 13. What is the area of the rectangle?

(A) 46   (B) 92   (C) 36   (D) 100   (E) 90

Problem 12. Given that all of the angles below are right angles, find the number of centimeters in the perimeter of the polygon.

(A) 136   (B) 129   (C) 125   (D) 126   (E) 128

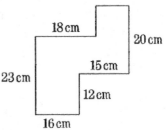

Problem 13. If the perimeter of trapezoid *ABCD* is 42 cm, what is the number of square centimeters in its area?

(A) 120   (B) 100   (C) 140   (D) 98   (E) 106

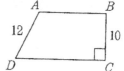

Problem 14. As shown in the figure, the area of trapezoid *ABCD* is 36. What is the length of *FB*?

(A) 8   (B) 2   (C) 4   (D) 3   (E) 5

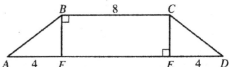

Problem 15. Trapezoid *ACDE* has bases of lengths 16cm and 20 cm and area of 180 square centimeters. Δ*BDE* has the longer base of the trapezoid as one of its sides. *B* lies on the other base. Find the number of square centimeters in the area of Δ*EBD*.

(A) 200   (B) 140   (C) 100   (D) 180   (E) 120

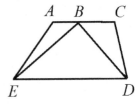

Problem 16. Find the area of a rhombus whose diagonals have length 4 and 9.

(A) 18   (B) 36   (C) 25   (D) 100   (E) 40

Problem 17. What is the radius of a circle whose perimeter is 64π cm?
(A) 64   (B) 32   (C) 16   (D) 8   (E) 128

Problem 18. If the circumference of a circle is 8π, what is its area?
(A) 16π (B) 18π (C) 20π (D) 64π (E) 49π

Problem 19. In the figure, the center of the circle is O and $\overline{AB}$ is tangent to the circle at point B. What is the area of the shaded region?

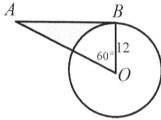

(A) $36\sqrt{3} - 24\pi$ (B) $36\sqrt{3} - 12\pi$
(C) $72\sqrt{3} - 12\pi$ (D) $72\sqrt{3} - 24\pi$
(E) $36\sqrt{3} - 12\pi$

Problem 20. $\overline{OA}$ is the diameter of the smaller circle and the radius of the larger circle. How many square units are in the area of the shaded region?
(A) 16π (B) 8π (C) 4π (D) 2π (E) π

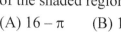

Problem 21. Isosceles right triangle ABC has legs of length 4cm with midpoints D and E. Three circles with centers A, B and C, respectively are drawn and the regions inside the triangle are shown. How many square centimeters are in the area of the shaded region?
(A) $16 - \pi$ (B) $16 - 2\pi$ (C) $8 - 2\pi$
(D) $8 - \pi$ (E) 8

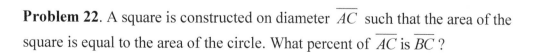

Problem 22. A square is constructed on diameter $\overline{AC}$ such that the area of the square is equal to the area of the circle. What percent of $\overline{AC}$ is $\overline{BC}$?

(A) $\dfrac{\sqrt{\pi}}{2}$ (B) $\dfrac{\pi}{2}$ (C) $\dfrac{3}{4}$ (D) $\dfrac{3\pi}{4}$ (E) $2 - \dfrac{\pi}{2}$

Problem 23. The length of a side of equilateral triangle ABC is 2. D, E, and F are the midpoints of $\overline{AB}$, $\overline{BC}$, and $\overline{AC}$, respectively. A, B, and C are the centers of the circles that contain arcs DF, DE, and FE, respectively. What is the area of the shaded region?

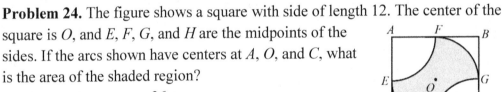

(A) $3\sqrt{2} - \dfrac{\pi}{2}$ (B) $\pi - \sqrt{3}$

(C) $2\sqrt{3} - \dfrac{\pi}{2}$ (D) $\sqrt{3} - \dfrac{\pi}{4}$

(E) $\sqrt{3} - \dfrac{\pi}{2}$

Problem 24. The figure shows a square with side of length 12. The center of the square is O, and E, F, G, and H are the midpoints of the sides. If the arcs shown have centers at A, O, and C, what is the area of the shaded region?

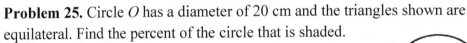

(A) 72   (B) $36 + \dfrac{36\pi}{7}$ (C) $18\pi - 18$

(D) 12π (E) $36 - 12\pi$

Problem 25. Circle O has a diameter of 20 cm and the triangles shown are equilateral. Find the percent of the circle that is shaded.

(A) $\dfrac{1}{2} - \dfrac{3\sqrt{3}}{2\pi}$ (B) $\dfrac{1}{2} - \dfrac{\sqrt{3}}{4\pi}$ (C) $\dfrac{1}{2} - \dfrac{\sqrt{3}}{\pi}$

(D) $\dfrac{1}{2} - \dfrac{3\sqrt{3}}{4\pi}$ (E) $\dfrac{1}{2} - \dfrac{3\sqrt{3}}{\pi}$

Problem 26. As shown in the figure, right triangle ABC with $BC = 20$ *cm*. BDC is a half circle with the diameter BC. The difference between two shaded areas I and II is 23. Find AC in terms of π.

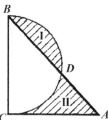

☆**Problem 27.** A circle of radius 4 is inscribed in a semicircle, as shown. The area inside the semicircle but outside the circle is shaded. What fraction of the semicircle's area is shaded?

(A) $\dfrac{1}{2}$ (B) $\dfrac{5\pi}{6}$ (C) $\dfrac{2}{\pi}$ (D) $\dfrac{2\pi}{3}$ (E) $\dfrac{3}{\pi}$.

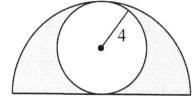

☆ **Problem 28.** In trapezoid $ABCD$, AD is perpendicular to DC, $AD = AB = 4$, and $DC = 8$. In addition, E is on DC, and BE is parallel to AD. Find the area of $\triangle BEC$.

(A) 4   (B) 8   (C) 12   (D) 18   (E) 10

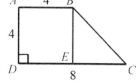

SOLUTION

Problem 1. Solution: C.

Method 1:

The shaded area / the rectangle area

$$= \frac{\frac{1}{2}L \times H}{LH} = 0.5 = 50\%.$$

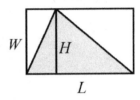

Method 2:

Let F be the midpoint of DC. Connect FA and FB.

Then $S_{\triangle ABE} = S_{\triangle ABF} = \frac{1}{2}S_{\triangle ABCD} \cdot \frac{S_{\triangle ABF}}{S_{\triangle ABCD}} = \frac{1}{2} = 50\%$

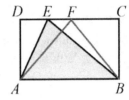

Problem 2. Solution: B.

The area of $\triangle ABD$ is half of the area of rectangle $ABCD$.

The answer is 24/2 = 12.

Problem 3. Solution: A.

Draw $FB \perp AC$. We know that $S_{\triangle ABE} = S_{\triangle FBE}$ and

$S_{\triangle BCD} = S_{\triangle BFD}$.

Thus the area of the shaded region is $\frac{1}{2}S_{ABCD} = \frac{1}{2} \times 4 \times 8 = 16$.

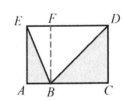

Problem 4. Solution: B.

Each side is 60/3 = 20. $A = \frac{1}{4}a^2\sqrt{3} = \frac{1}{4} \times 20^2\sqrt{3} = 100\sqrt{3}$

Problem 5. Solution: B.

Method 1: Area of a triangle with sides a, b, and c (Heron Formula):

$A = \sqrt{s(s-a)(s-b)(s-c)}$, where $s = \frac{1}{2}(a+b+c) = 15$.

$A = \sqrt{15(15-5)(15-12)(15-13)}$

$= \sqrt{15 \times 10 \times 3 \times 2} = \sqrt{3 \times 5 \times 2 \times 5 \times 3 \times 2} = 2 \times 5 \times 3 = 30$

Method 2:

The triangle is a right triangle with two legs of 5 and 12. The area is

$A = \frac{1}{2}b \times h = \frac{1}{2} \times 5 \times 12 = 30$.

Problem 6. Solution: B.

Method 1: Area of a triangle with sides a, b, and c (Heron Formula):

$A = \sqrt{s(s-a)(s-b)(s-c)}$, where $s = \frac{1}{2}(a+b+c) = 20$.

$A = \sqrt{20(20-8)(20-15)(20-17)}$

$= \sqrt{20 \times 12 \times 5 \times 3} = \sqrt{4^2 \times 5^2 \times 3^2} = 4 \times 5 \times 3 = 60$

Method 2:

The triangle is a right triangle with two legs of 8 and 15. The area is

$A = \frac{1}{2}b \times h = \frac{1}{2} \times 8 \times 15 = 60$.

Problem 7. Solution: A.

Let x be the area of the region D.

$35 \times 36 = 45 \times x \qquad \Rightarrow \qquad x = 28$.

$35 + 36 + 45 + 28 = 144$.

Problem 8. Solution: B.

Method 1 (official solution):

Slide triangle A down to fill in triangle B. The resulting 2 × 3 rectangle has area 6.

Method 2 (our solution):

By **Pick's Law**, $Area = \dfrac{12}{2} + 1 - 1 = 6$.

Problem 9. Solution: A.

$8 \times 2 + 7 \times 2 + 4 \times 2 = 38$.

Problem 10. Solution: A.

A good way to solve this problem is to move two red colored sides to each end. (Note the area does increase for the new figure by a part of $11 \times 12 = 131$ square units). After doing that, a rectangle is formed with known side lengths.

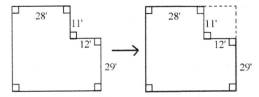

The area of new figure is $A = L \times W = (28 + 12) \times (29 + 11) = 40 \times 40 = 1600$. The area of the original figure is then $1600 - 132 = 1468$.

Problem 11. Solution: E.

Let x be the length and y be the width.

$2(x + y) = 46$ (1)

$x - y = 13$ (2)

$(1) + 2 \times (2)$: $4x = 72$ $\Rightarrow$ $x = 18$

So $y = 5$. The area is $18 \times 5 = 90$ (units^2).

Problem 12. Solution: D.

$2 \times (16 + 15) + 2 \times (20 + 12) = 62 + 64 = 126$.

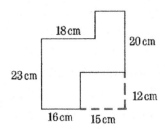

Problem 13. Solution: B.

Perimeter of a trapezoid: $P = b_1 + b_2 + c + d$

$\Rightarrow \quad 42 = b_1 + b_2 + 12 + 10$

$b_1 + b_2 = 42 - 12 - 10 = 20$

So the area of the trapezoid: $A = \dfrac{(b_1 + b_2)}{2}h = \dfrac{20}{2} \times 10 = 100$ (cm^2).

Problem 14. Solution: D.

The area of the trapezoid is $36 = \dfrac{(8 + 4 + 8 + 4)}{2} \times BF \qquad \Rightarrow \qquad BF = 3$.

Problem 15. Solution: C.

The area of the trapezoid is $180 = \dfrac{(16 + 20)}{2} \times BF$.

$BF = \dfrac{180 \times 2}{16 + 20} = 10$

The area of the shaded region $S_{\triangle EDB} = \dfrac{1}{2} \times 20 \times 10 = 100$

cm^2.

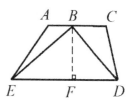

Problem 16. Solution: A.

Area of a rhombus: $A = \dfrac{1}{2}d_1 \times d_2 = \dfrac{1}{2} \times 4 \times 9 = 2 \times 9 = 18$ (units^2).

Problem 17. Solution: B.

$C = 2\pi r \qquad \Rightarrow \qquad 64\pi = 2\pi \times r \quad \Rightarrow \quad r = 32$ cm.

Problem 18. Solution: A.

$C = 2\pi r \qquad \Rightarrow \qquad 8\pi = 2\pi \times r \quad \Rightarrow \quad 4 = r$

$A = \pi r^2 = \pi \times 4^2 = 16\pi$ (units^2).

Problem 19. Solution: D.

$\triangle ABO$ is a $30° - 60° - 9°0$ right triangle. So $AB = 12\sqrt{3}$.

$S_{\triangle ABO} = \dfrac{1}{2} \times 12\sqrt{3} \times 12 = 72\sqrt{3}$.

The shaded area is $S_{\triangle ABO} - \dfrac{1}{6} S_O = 72\sqrt{3} - \dfrac{1}{6} \times \pi \times (12)^2 = 72\sqrt{3} - 24\pi$.

Problem 20. Solution: D.

The shaded area = the area of quarter-circle of radius 4 – the area of semi-circle of radius 2.

The answer is $\dfrac{1}{4} \times \pi \times (4)^2 - \dfrac{1}{2} \times \pi \times (2)^2 = 4\pi - 2\pi = 2\pi$.

Problem 21. Solution: C.

Shaded area = the area of triangle $ABC -$ (the area of sector $ADG +$ the area of sector $CEF +$ the area of sector BDE) =

$\dfrac{1}{2} AB \times BC - (\dfrac{45}{360} \times \pi \times AD^2 + \dfrac{45}{360} \times \pi \times CE^2 + \dfrac{90}{360} \times \pi \times DB^2)$

$= \dfrac{1}{2} \times 4 \times 4 - (\dfrac{45}{360} \times \pi \times 2^2 + \dfrac{45}{360} \times \pi \times 2^2 + \dfrac{90}{360} \times \pi \times 2^2)$

$= 8 - 4\pi(\dfrac{45}{360} + \dfrac{45}{360} + \dfrac{90}{360}) = 8 - 2\pi$.

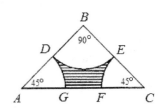

Problem 22. Solution: A.

Let AB be m, the radius of the circle be r.

We have $(2r - m)^2 = \pi r^2$ $\Rightarrow$ $2r - m = \sqrt{\pi} r \Rightarrow$

$\qquad m = 2r - \sqrt{\pi} r$

$\dfrac{BC}{AC} = \dfrac{2r - m}{2r} = 1 - \dfrac{m}{2r} = 1 - \dfrac{2r - \sqrt{\pi} r}{2r} = 1 - (1 - \dfrac{\sqrt{\pi}}{2}) = \dfrac{\sqrt{\pi}}{2}$.

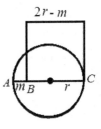

Problem 23. Solution: E.

Shaded area = the area of triangle ABC – (the area of sector ADF + the area of sector CEF + the area of sector BDE)

= the area of triangle ABC – 3 × (the area of sector ADF) =

$$\frac{\sqrt{3}}{4} \times 2^2 - 3 \times (\frac{60}{360} \times \pi \times AD^2) = \sqrt{3} - 3 \times (\frac{60}{360} \times \pi \times 1^2) = \sqrt{3} - \frac{\pi}{2}.$$

Problem 24. Solution: A.

$$a = S_{ABCD} - 4 \times \frac{1}{4} \pi \times AF^2 = 12^2 - 4 \times \frac{1}{4} \pi \times 6^2 = 144 - 36\pi.$$

$$b = \frac{1}{4}(S_{circle} - a) = \frac{1}{4}(\pi \times 6^2 - 144 + 36\pi) = 18\pi - 36.$$

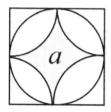 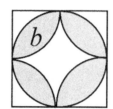

The area of the shaded region = $a + 2b = 144 - 36\pi + 2(18\pi - 36) = 72$.

Problem 25. Solution: D.

The shaded area in the figure below = the area of sector OAB – the area of equilateral triangle OAB =

$$\frac{1}{6} \times \pi \times AO^2 - \frac{\sqrt{3}}{4} \times AO^2 = \frac{1}{6} \times \pi \times 10^2 - \frac{\sqrt{3}}{4} \times 10^2$$

$$= \frac{50}{3} \times \pi - 25\sqrt{3}.$$

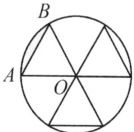

The percent of the circle that is shaded is

$$\frac{3(\frac{1}{6} \times \pi \times 10^2 - \frac{\sqrt{3}}{4} \times 100)}{\pi \times 10^2} = \frac{1}{2} - \frac{\frac{3\sqrt{3}}{4}}{\pi} = \frac{1}{2} - \frac{3\sqrt{3}}{4\pi}.$$

Problem 26. Solution: $\dfrac{50\pi + 23}{10}$.

Let $AC = x$, $S_{\triangle ABC}$ be the area of triangle ABC, and S_{BDC} be the area of half circle BDC.

From the diagram to the right, we see that

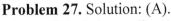

$$S_{\triangle ABC} = S_{III} + S_{II} \qquad\qquad (1)$$

$$S_{BDC} = S_{III} + S_{I} \qquad\qquad (2)$$

$(1) - (2)$: $S_{\triangle ABC} - S_{BDC} = S_{II} - S_{I} = 23$

$$= \frac{1}{2} \cdot 20x - \frac{\pi}{2} \cdot 10^2 = 10x - 50\pi.$$

Or $10x - 50\pi = 23 \quad\Rightarrow\quad x = \dfrac{50\pi + 23}{10}$.

Problem 27. Solution: (A).
The semicircle has radius 4 and total area

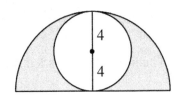

$\dfrac{1}{2} \times \pi \times 8^2 = 32\pi$. The area of the circle is

$\pi \times 4^2 = 16\pi$. The fraction of the area that is not

shaded is $\dfrac{16\pi}{32\pi} = \dfrac{1}{2}$, and hence the fraction of the area

that is shaded is also $\dfrac{1}{2}$.

☆ **Problem 28.** Solution: B.
The area of the $\triangle BEC$ is the area of the trapezoid $ABCD$
minus the area of the square $ABED$. The area of $\triangle BEC$ is

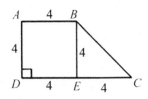

$$A = \frac{(4+8)}{2} \times 4 - 4^2 = 24 - 16 = 8.$$

BASIC KNOWLEDGE AND TERMS

Each pattern is created and arranged following a rule or rules. The key for solving pattern problems is to identify the core of the patterns.

Typical AMC 8/Mathcounts pattern problems can be classified as the following:

Growing patterns: Growing patterns have a sequence of elements that increase or decrease systematically when viewed as a recursive pattern.

Sequences pattern: Sequences pattern is a pattern of an ordered set of numbers or mathematical entities.

Repeating patterns: Repeating patterns can be generalized by recognizing pattern families that can look different but have the same core.

Geometric Patterns: A geometric pattern is a pattern that has repeating shapes such as dots, lines, triangles, circle, rectangles, and polygons.

USEFUL FORMULAS

Arithmetic sequence:

If any two consecutive terms in a sequence $a_1, a_2, a_3, \ldots, a_n, \ldots$, have the same difference, the sequence is an arithmetic sequence.
The difference is called the common difference.

$$d = a_{n+1} - a_n$$

The nth term is expressed as

$$a_n = a_1 + (n-1)d$$

The sum of n terms in the sequence:

$$S = na_1 + \frac{(n-1)d}{2}n \quad \text{or} \quad S = \frac{(a_1 + a_n)n}{2}.$$

Newton's Little Formula for n^{th} term:

For an arithmetic sequence of high order:

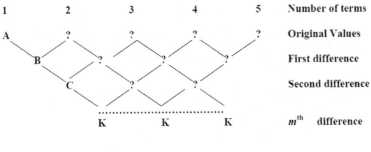

$$a_n = A\binom{n-1}{0} + B\binom{n-1}{1} + C\binom{n-1}{2} + \cdots\cdots + K\binom{n-1}{m}$$

Geometric sequence

If any two consecutive terms in a sequence a_1, a_2, a_3, ..., a_n,..., have the same ratio, the sequence is called a geometric sequence (or geometric progression).

a_1 is the **first term**.

a_n is the **general term** or n^{th} term. $a_n = a_1 \cdot q^{n-1}$

The same ratio is called the **common ratio** (q or r).

The sum of the first n terms is expressed as S_n. For example, S_{12} means the sum of the first twelve terms.

$$S_n = \frac{a_1(1 - q^n)}{1 - q}.$$

GROWING PATTERNS

Example 1. Consider the following pattern:

$$\sqrt{1+1\cdot2\cdot3\cdot4}=5$$
$$\sqrt{1+2\cdot3\cdot4\cdot5}=11$$
$$\sqrt{1+3\cdot4\cdot5\cdot6}=19$$
$$\sqrt{1+4\cdot5\cdot6\cdot7}=29$$

Find $\sqrt{1+50\cdot51\cdot52\cdot53}$

(A) 2550   (B) 2651   (C) 2652   (D) 2756   (E) 2703

Solution: B.

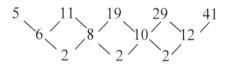

$$a_{50}=5\binom{49}{0}+6\binom{49}{1}+2\binom{49}{2}=5+294+2352=2651.$$

Example 2. If the same pattern is continued, what is the number of 1's in the result of the calculation in the eighth line of the pattern?

$1\times9+2=\underline{\hspace{2cm}}$

$12\times9+3=\underline{\hspace{2cm}}$

$123\times9+4=\underline{\hspace{2cm}}$

(A) 4   (B) 6   (C) 8   (D) 9   (E) 10

Solution: D.

The rule is as follows:

First line: $1\times9+2=11$
Second line: $12\times9+3=111$
Third line: $123\times9+4=1111$

nth line: $12...n \times 9 + (n+1) = \underbrace{11\cdot\cdot11}_{n+1' \ 1's}$

Eighth line: $12345678 \times 9 + (8+1) = 111,111,111$. The answer is D.

Example 3. Look for a pattern in the following and then determine the value of n:

$$121 = \frac{22 \times 22}{1+2+1}$$

$$12321 = \frac{333 \times 333}{1+2+3+2+1}$$

$$n = \frac{4444 \times 4444}{1+2+3+4+3+2+1}$$

The sum of the digits of n is:

(A) 14   (B) 16   (C) 18   (D) 19   (E) 20

Solution: B.

The pattern is

$$\underbrace{12\cdots n\cdots 21}_{2n-1\,digits} = \frac{\overbrace{n\cdots n}^{n'n\ s} \times \overbrace{n\cdots n}^{n'n\ s}}{\underbrace{1+2+\cdots n\cdots +2+1}_{2n-1\,numbers}}$$

$$\frac{4444 \times 4444}{1+2+3+4+3+2+1} = 1234321 = 1,234,321.$$ The answer is 16.

Example 4. Use the pattern given to express 100^2 in the form $a^2 + b^2 - c^2$. What is the value $a + b + c$?

$12^2 = 8^2 + 9^2 - 1^2$
$14^2 = 10^2 + 10^2 - 2^2$
$16^2 = 12^2 + 11^2 - 3^2$
$18^2 = 14^2 + 12^2 - 4^2$

(A) 198   (B) 153   (C) 145   (D) 196   (E) 194

Solution: E.

Let $d^2 = a^2 + b^2 - c^2$

| d: 12, 14, 16, …, 100 | $\Rightarrow$ | $100 = 12 + (n-1) \times 2$ | $\Rightarrow n = 45.$ |

a: 8, 10, 12, …, a	$\Rightarrow$	$a = 8 + (n-1) \times 2$	$\Rightarrow a = 96.$
b: 9, 10, 11, …, b	$\Rightarrow$	$b = 9 + (n-1) \times 2$	$\Rightarrow b = 53.$
c: 1, 2, 3, …, c	$\Rightarrow$	$c = 1 + (n-1) \times 1$	$\Rightarrow c = 45.$

$a + b + c = 96 + 53 + 45 = 194.$

Example 5. The first three towers in a sequence are shown. The nth tower is formed by stacking n blocks on top of an $n \times n$ square of blocks. How many blocks are in the 99th tower?

(A) 9900   (B) 9816   (C) 9818   (D) 9919   (E) 9801

Solution: A.

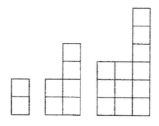

The pattern is $1 \times 1 + 1,\ 2 \times 2 + 2,\ 3 \times 3 + 3, …,\ n \times n + n.$

The number of blocks in 99th tower is $n \times n + n = 99 \times 99 + 99 = 99\,(99 + 1) = 9900$

Example 6. The first three hexagonal numbers are represented as shown. Find the sum of the first five hexagonal numbers.

(A) 44   (B) 45   (C) 48   (D) 39   (E) 50

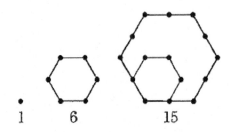

1   6   15

Solution: B.

The pattern is $1, 1 + 5, 1 + 5 + (4 \times 3 - 3),\ 1 + 5 + (4 \times 3 - 3) + (4 \times 4 - 3) = 28,$
$1 + 5 + (4 \times 3 - 3) + (4 \times 4 - 3) + (4 \times 5 - 3) = 45.$

Note the general formula can be written as

$$a_n = 1 + 5 + \sum_{i=3}^{n}(4 \times i - 3),\ \text{or } 2n^2 - n.$$

SEQUENCES PATTERN

☆**Example 7.** Terri produces a sequence of positive integers by following three rules. She starts with a positive integer, then applies the appropriate rule to the result, and continues in this fashion.
Rule 1: If the integer is less than 10, multiply it by 9.
Rule 2: If the integer is even and greater than 9, divide it by 2.
Rule 3: If the integer is odd and greater than 9, subtract 5 from it.

A sample sequence: 23, 18, 9, 81, 76, ...
Find the 198th term of the sequence that begins 49, 44. . . .
(A) 54   (B) 6   (C) 22   (D) 49   (E) 11

Solution: C.

The sequence is 49, 44, 22, 11, 6, 54, 27, 22, ... After 2 terms the cycle (22, 11, 6, 54, 27) is repeated. The repeating cycle is five terms. The 198th term is the 196th term in the new sequence. $196 = 5 \times 39 + 1$. So 195th term is the same as the first term in the new cycle, and this is 22.

Example 8. All positive integers appear in the sequence 1, 2, 2, 3, 3, 3, 4, 4, 4, 4, . . ., and each positive integer k appears in the sequence k times. In the sequence, each term after the first is greater than or equal to each of the terms before it. If the integer 12 first appears in the sequence as the nth term, what is the value of n?
(A) 64   (B) 67   (C) 65   (D) 66   (E) 62

Solution: B.
The integer 11 will appear 11 times. The last one of the integer 11 appears as the 66th term because $\dfrac{(1+11)\times 11}{2} = 66$.

So the integer 12 first appears in the sequence as the 67th term.

Example 9. Complete the pattern: 10, 15, 22.5, 33.75, ———
(A) 44.85   (B) 55.95   (C) 40.675   (D) 50.625   (E) 50

Solution: D.
The pattern shows that these terms form a geometric sequence with the common ratio 1.5.
$$\frac{x}{33.75} = \frac{15}{10} \quad \Rightarrow \quad x = 50.625 .$$

Example 10. The first term of a sequence is 5 and each subsequent term is 5 less than twice the preceding term. What is the eighth term?
(A) 5   (B) 6   (C) 2   (D) 4   (E) 8

Solution: A.
We list some of the terms:
$5, 2 \times 5 - 5 = 5, \ 2 \times 5 - 5 = 5, \ \ldots$
We see that this is a constant sequence of 5.

Example 11. What is the 50th letter in this pattern: $ABCAABBCCAAABBBCCC$ . ...?
(A) A (B) B (C) C (D) D (E) E

Solution: *A.*

We separate the sequence as *ABC, AABBCC, AAABBBCCC, . .*

We get 3, 6, 9, 12, 15, 18, 21,…

$3 + 6 + 9 + 12 + 15 = 45$.

The next $18/3 = 6$ terms will be the letter *A*. So the 50th letter in this pattern is *A*.

Example 12. A sequence is formed by writing the word COMPETITIONS over and over again. What is the 496th letter in this sequence?

(A) C   (B) O   (C) M   (D) P   (E) E

Solution: D.

We see that pattern repeats every 12 letters. $496 = 12 \times 41 + 4$.

So the 496th letter in this sequence is P.

Example 13. The sequence 0, 1, 2, 2, 3, 3, 0, 1, 2, 2, 3, 3, . . .repeats every six terms. The first term is 0. What is the 998th term?

(A) 0   (B) 1   (C) 2   (D) 3   (E) 998

Solution: B.

0, 1, 2, 2, 3, 3,

0, 1, 2, 2, 3, 3,

. .

$998 = 6 \times 166 + 2$.

The 998th term is the same as the second term in the pattern, that is 1.

Example 14. The first six terms of a sequence are 1, –2, 3, –4, 5, –6. . . .. The odd-numbered terms are increasing consecutive positive odd integers starting with 1. The even-numbered terms are decreasing consecutive negative even integers starting with –2. What is the sum of the 50th and 51st terms of the sequence?

(A) –101   (B) –1   (C) 0   (D) 1   (E) 101

Solution: D.

We see the pattern that the sum of every two consecutive numbers is
$a_{2n} + a_{2m+1} = 1$ and $a_{2n+1} + a_{2m+2} = -1$.
So $a_{50} + a_{51} = 1$

REPEATING PATTERNS

Repeating patterns can be generalized by recognizing pattern families that can look different but have the same core.

Example 15. What is the 100th digit of the decimal representation of $\frac{1}{7}$?

(A) 1   (B) 4   (C) 2   (D) 8   (E) 7

Solution: D.

$\frac{1}{7} = 0.\overline{142857}$. The pattern repeats every 6 digits.

$100 = 16 \times 6 + 4.$

Thus the 100th digit is the same as the 4th digit in the pattern, which is 8.

Example 16. What is the 17th digit after the decimal point in the decimal expansion of $\frac{11}{7}$?

(A) 5   (B) 4   (C) 2   (D) 8   (E) 7

Solution: C.

$\frac{11}{7} = 1 + \frac{4}{7}$. The 17th digit after the decimal point in the decimal expansion is determined by $\frac{4}{7}$ only.

$\frac{4}{7} = 0.\overline{571428}$. The pattern repeats every 6 digits.

$17 = 2 \times 6 + 5.$

Thus the 17th digit is the same as the 5th digit, which is 2.

Example 17. What is the $123,999^{th}$ digit after the decimal in the decimal expansion of $\dfrac{123}{999}$?

(A) 1　　　　　(B) 2　　　　　(C) 3　　　　　(D) 4　　　　　(E) 9

Solution: C.

$\dfrac{123}{999} = \dfrac{41}{333} = 0.\overline{123}$.

The pattern repeats every 3 digits.

$123,999 = 41,333 \times 3$.

Thus the $123,999^{th}$ digit is the same as the last digit, which is 3.

Example 18. Starting with a green bead, colored beads are placed on a string according to the pattern green, red, blue, yellow, white, orange. If this pattern is repeated, what is the color of the 51st bead?

(A) Green　　　(B) Red　　　(C) Blue　　　(D) Yellow　　　(E) White

Solution: C

The pattern repeats every 6 colors in the order of green, red, blue, yellow, white, orange.

$51 = 8 \times 6 + 3$.

Thus the 51st bead is the same as the 3rd bead, which is blue.

Example 19. The table shown shows Pythagorean triples for which $c = b + 1$. Find the value of c when $a = 15$.

a	b	c
3	4	5
5	12	13
7	24	25
9	40	41

(A) 110   (B) 111   (C) 112   (D) 113   (E) 115

Solution: D.

The pattern for b:

Thus $c = b + 1 = 112 + 1 = 113$.

Example 20. The whole numbers are written consecutively in rows as shown. Each row contains two more numbers than the previous row. What is the number of the row in which the number 1,300 is listed?

Row 1					0			
Row 2				1	2	3		
Row 3			8	7	6	5	4	
Row 4		9	10	11	12	13	14	15
Row 5	24	23	22	21	20	19	18	17	16

(A) 35   (B) 36   (C) 37   (D) 38   (E) 39

Solution: C.

We know that $1 + 3 + 5 + ... + (2n - 1) = n^2$.

Since 1,300 is the $1,300 + 1 = 1,301^{st}$ number. $1296 = 36^2 < 1301 < 37^2 = 1369$. We know that the last number in the 36 row is $1296 - 1 = 1295$. The first number in 37 row is $1297 - 1 = 1296$ and the last number in that row is $1396 - 1 = 1395$. So $1,301^{st}$ number must be in the 37th row.

Example 21. The lattice shown is continued for 100 rows. What will be the third number in the 100th row?

Row 1:	1	2	3	4	5	6	7
Row 2:	8	9	10	11	12	13	14
Row 3:	15	16	17	18	19	20	21
Row 4:	22	23	24	25	26	27	28

(A) 696   (B) 695   (C) 697   (D) 694   (E) 99

Solution: A.

We see a pattern for every 7 integers in the table.

The last number is the 99th row is $99 \times 7 = 693$.

So the first number in the 100th row is 694, the second number in the 100th row is 695, and the third number in the 100th row is 696.

GEOMETRIC PATTERNS

Example 22. Referring to the sketches, it is seen that 3, 9, and 18 matches are required to make the triangular patterns depicted, respectively. How many matches would be needed to construct a similar figure with a ten match-stick base?

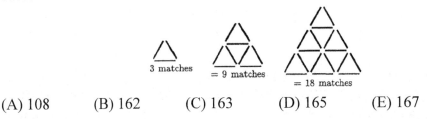

3 matches

= 9 matches

= 18 matches

(A) 108   (B) 162   (C) 163   (D) 165   (E) 167

Solution: D.

$$3 \quad\nearrow\quad 9 \quad\nearrow\quad 18 \quad\nearrow\quad 30$$
$$\searrow 6 \nearrow \quad \searrow 9 \quad \searrow 12 \nearrow$$
$$\searrow 3 \nearrow \quad \searrow 3 \nearrow$$

By the Newton's Little Formula $a_{50} = 3\binom{9}{0} + 6\binom{9}{1} + 3\binom{9}{2} = 3 + 54 + 108 = 165$.

Example 23. The diagram shows an arrangement of 10 cubes in 3 layers. How many cubes will it take to make 8 layers?
(A) 116   (B) 118   (C) 120   (D) 124   (E) 144

Solution: 120 (cubes)
We are looking for a pattern:

Layers:	1 layer	2 layers	3 layers	4 layers
#of cubes:	1	$1 \times 2 + 2 \times 1$	$1 \times 3 + 2 \times 2 + 3 \times 1$	$1 \times 4 + 2 \times 3$

$+ 3 \times 2 + 4 \times 1$
The number of cubes will it take to make 8 layers:
$1 \times 8 + 2 \times 7 + 3 \times 6 + 4 \times 5 + 5 \times 4 + 6 \times 3 + 7 \times 2 + 8 \times 1 = 120$.

Example 24. By continuing the pattern shown, how many non-overlapping triangles would appear in the last figure?

(A) 36   (B) 38   (C) 40   (D) 44   (E) 99

Solution: C.
The pattern is
1, $1 + 1 \times 3$, $1 + 1 \times 3 + 3 \times 3$, $1 + 1 \times 3 + 3 \times 3 + 9 \times 3 = 40$.

Example 25. Each time a change occurs, the central one-fourth of every white equilateral triangle is shaded. What fractional part of the original equilateral triangle would be shaded after four changes? Express your answer as a common fraction.

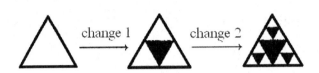

(A) $\dfrac{175}{256}$ (B) $\dfrac{173}{256}$ (C) $\dfrac{43}{64}$ (D) $\dfrac{177}{256}$ (E) $\dfrac{41}{256}$

Solution: A.

Step	fractional part
Change 1	1/4
2	$1/4 + 3 \times (1/4)^2$.
3	$1/4 + 3 \times (1/4)^2 + 3^2 \times (1/4)^3$
4	$1/4 + 3 \times (1/4)^2 + 3^2 \times (1/4)^3 + 3^3 \times (1/4)^4$

The answer is $\dfrac{175}{256}$.

Example 26. Thirty-six cannon balls are placed on a flat surface in the shape of a square to form the base of a display beside the cannon. How many additional cannonballs are needed to form a "pyramid" with the given square base?

(A) 55   (B) 91   (C) 40   (D) 36   (E) 99

Solution: A.

The pattern is $6 \times 6, 5 \times 5, 4 \times 4, 3 \times 3, 2 \times 2, 1 \times 1$.

Total number of cannon balls is $36 + 25 + 16 + 9 + 2 + 1 = 91$. The answer is $91 - 36 = 55$.

☆**Example 27.** Points B, D, and J are midpoints of the sides of right triangle ACG. Points K, E, I are midpoints of the sides of triangle JDG, etc. If the dividing and shading process is done 101 times (the first three are shown) and $AC = CG = 12$, then the total area of the shaded triangles is nearest to

(A) 24   (B) 12   (C) 18   (D) 19   (E) 20

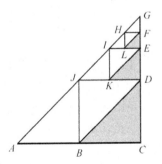

Solution: (A).

At each stage the area of the shaded triangle is one-third of the trapezoidal region not containing the smaller triangle being divided in the next step. Thus, the total area of the shaded triangles comes closer and closer to one-third of the area of the triangular region ACG and this is $1/3 \times 1/2 \times 12 \times 12 = 24$.

Example 28. A grocer stacks apples in the shape of a square pyramid. The bottom layer is a 10×10 square, the top layer is one apple, and the nth layer is an $n \times n$ square. How many apples does she have in the pyramid?

(A) 368   (B) 385   (C) 340   (D) 440   (E) 399

Solution: B.

The pattern is 10×10, 9×9, $8 \times 8,\ldots, 1 \times 1$.

The answer is $\dfrac{n(n+1)}{2} \times \dfrac{2n+1}{3} = \dfrac{10(10+1)}{2} \times \dfrac{2 \times 10+1}{3} = 385$

Note: $1^1 + 2^2 + 3^2 + \ldots + n^2 = \dfrac{n(n+1)}{2} \times \dfrac{2n+1}{3}$.

PROBLEMS

Problem 1. Find the numerical value x_8, if

$x_0 = 1^0$

$x_1 = 2^0 + 2^1$

$x_2 = 4^0 + 4^{\frac{1}{2}} + 4^1$

$x_3 = 8^0 + 8^{\frac{1}{3}} + 8^{\frac{2}{3}} + 8^1$

$x_4 = 16^0 + 16^{\frac{1}{4}} + 16^{\frac{1}{2}} + 16^{\frac{3}{4}} + 16^1$

(A) 512   (B) 511   (C) 256   (D) 1024   (E) 1023

Problem 2. Look for a pattern:

$$11 \times 11 = 121$$
$$111 \times 111 = 12321$$
$$1111 \times 1111 = 1234321$$

Find the value of n: $111111 \times 111111 = n$

Problem 3. Look for a pattern:

$1^3 = 1^2 - 0^2$

$2^3 = 3^2 - 1^2$

$3^3 = 6^2 - 3^2$

$$\vdots$$

$6^3 = n^2 - m^2$

What is the value of $m + n$?

Problem 4. Follow the pattern to determine the value of $8(23456789) + 9$.

$$8(2) + 2 = 18$$
$$8(23) + 3 = 187$$
$$8(234) + 4 = 1876$$
$$8(2345) + 5 = 18765$$
$$8(23456) + 6 = 187654$$

Problem 5. The first figure contains 2 dots, the second 6 dots, and the third 12 dots. If the pattern continues, how many dots would the tenth figure contain?

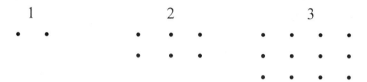

Problem 6. Each arrangement of squares is formed from the preceding arrangement by adding two additional squares to each end of the horizontal row and one square to the vertical column. How many squares will be in the sixth figure in the sequence?

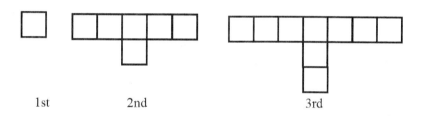

Problem 7. If the pattern continues, what is the next term in the sequence 1, 7, 25, 61, 121, . . . ?

Problem 8. Complete the pattern: 40.5, 9, 2, —————

Problem 9. Find the next decimal term in the sequence:

0, 0.5, $0.\overline{6}$, 0.75, . . .

Problem 10. What is the 100th letter in the pattern *ABCABCABC* . . . ?

Problem 11. The sequence shown was formed by writing the first letter of the alphabet followed by writing the first two letters of the alphabet and continuing the pattern by writing one more letter of the alphabet each time. Continuing this pattern, what letter is the 280th letter in this sequence?

   $A, A, B, A, B, C, A, B, C, D, A, B, C, D, E, \ldots$

Problem 12. A sequence of letters is formed by writing 1 A, 2 B's, 3 C's, and so forth, increasing the number of letters written by one each time the next letter of the alphabet is written. What is the 200th letter in the sequence?

Problem 13. Begin with the 200-digit number 987654321098765 . . . 543210, which repeats the digits 0-9 in reverse order. From the left, choose every third digit to form a new number. Repeat the same process with the new number. Continue the process repeatedly until the result is a two-digit number. What is the resulting two-digit number?

Problem 14. What is the 1997th digit to the right of the decimal point in the decimal expansion of $\frac{1}{7}$?

Problem 15. What is the 199th digit of the decimal representation of $\frac{3}{37}$?

Problem 16. What is the 125th digit beyond the decimal point in the decimal representation of $\frac{4}{7}$?

Problem 17. The positive odd integers are arranged in 5 columns, A, B, C, D, and E, continuing the pattern shown. In which column will 1599 appear?

A	B	C	D	E
	1	3	5	7
15	13	11	9	
	17	19	21	23
31	29	27	25	
	33	35	37	39
47	45	43	41	
	49	51	. . .	

Problem 18. The multiples of 3 are arranged in the following manner:

Column 1	Column 2	Column 3	Column 4
3	6	9	12
21	18	15	12
21	24	27	30
39	36	33	30
39	42	…	…

In which column will the number 1992 appear?

Problem 19. The natural numbers from 1 to 1,000 are arranged consecutively from left to right in a triangle as shown. Each row contains one more number than the row below. What number is directly above 723?

. . .

11	12	13	14	15
7	8	9	10	
4	5	6		
2	3			
1				

Problem 20. Triangular numbers can be represented by a triangular array. For example, 1, 3, and 6 can be represented as:

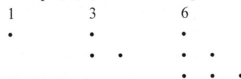

The difference of a pair of consecutive triangular numbers is 12. Find their sum.

Problem 21. Squares are used to build the following sequence of drawings. If the length of a side of each square is one unit, how many units are in the perimeter of the 8th drawing?

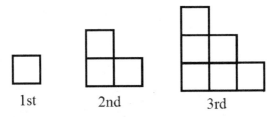

1st   2nd   3rd

Problem 22. At each stage the midpoints of the sides of each unshaded equilateral triangle are connected and the triangle formed is shaded. Continuing in this process, what is the number of the stage when the shaded area is first larger than 90% of the area of the original equilateral triangle?

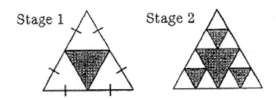

Stage 1   Stage 2

☆**Problem 23.** If the pattern in the diagram continues, what fraction of the interior would be shaded in the ninth triangle?

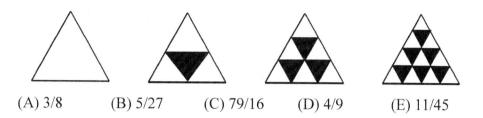

(A) 3/8   (B) 5/27   (C) 79/16   (D) 4/9   (E) 11/45

Problem 24. As you proceed from term to term, each shaded square is divided into four congruent squares and the upper left square of the four is painted white. By continuing the pattern, what fractional part of the tenth figure will be shaded? Express your answer as a common fraction in which the numerator and denominator are expressed in prime factored form using exponents.

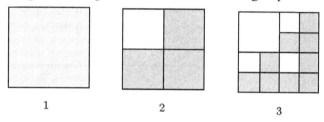

1   2   3

Problem 25. Each of the figures is a square formed by connecting midpoints of opposite sides of a larger square. What fraction of the largest square is shaded?

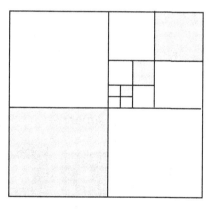

Problem 26. The first four triangular numbers are pictured. The *n*th triangular number is formed by drawing a row of *n* dots below the (*n* – 1)st triangular dot

pattern. The kth triangular number is represented by 120 dots. What is the value of k?

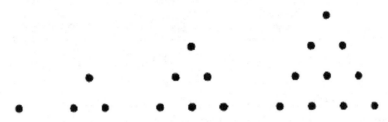

Problem 27. At each stage, the square at the lower left is divided into 4 congruent square regions, 2 of which are shaded. The area of the entire square (including shaded and unshaded parts) is 256 square units. How many square units are in the shaded area at the fifth stage? Express your answer as a decimal.

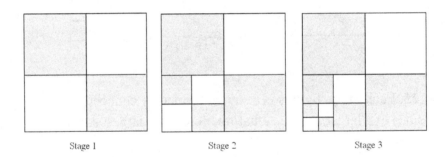

Stage 1   Stage 2   Stage 3

Problem 28. The "border number" of an $n \times n$ square is defined as the number of unit squares whose edges border the edges of a larger square. The border numbers of $1 \times 1, 2 \times 2, 3 \times 3, 4 \times 4$, and 5×5 squares are illustrated. What is the border number of a 20 unit by 20 unit square?

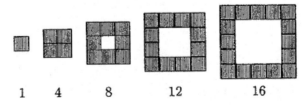

1   4   8   12   16

SOLUTIONS

Problem 1. Solution: B.

The rule is

$$x_n = (2^n)^{\frac{0}{n}} + (2^n)^{\frac{1}{n}} + (2^n)^{\frac{2}{n}} + (2^n)^{\frac{3}{n}} + \cdots + (2^n)^{\frac{n}{n}} =$$
$$(2)^0 + (2)^1 + (2)^2 + (2)^3 + \cdots + (2)^n$$
$$x_8 = (2)^0 + (2)^1 + (2)^2 + (2)^3 + \cdots + (2)^8 = 2^9 - 1 = 511.$$

Problem 2. Solution: 12,345,654,321

The rule is as follows:

$$11 \times 11 = 121$$
$$111 \times 111 = 12321$$
$$m' \text{ 1s} \times m' \text{ 1s} = 123\ldots(m-1)\,m\,(m-1)\ldots321$$

6' 1s:

$$111111 \times 111111 = 12345654321 = 12,345,654,321.$$

Problem 3. Solution: 36.

The pattern is as follows:

Left hand side: 1, 2, 3, 4, 5, 6.

Right hand side: Column 1: 1, 3, 6, 10, 15, 21; Column 2: 0, 1, 3, 6, 10, 15.

$$6^3 = 21^2 - 15^2$$
$$m + n = 21 + 15 = 36.$$

Problem 4. Solution: 187,654,321

The pattern is $8(\underbrace{23\ldots n}_{n \text{ digits}}) + n = 1\,\underbrace{8\ldots}_{n \text{ digits}}$.

$$8(23456789) + 9 = 187,654,321.$$

Problem 5. Solution: 110 (dots)

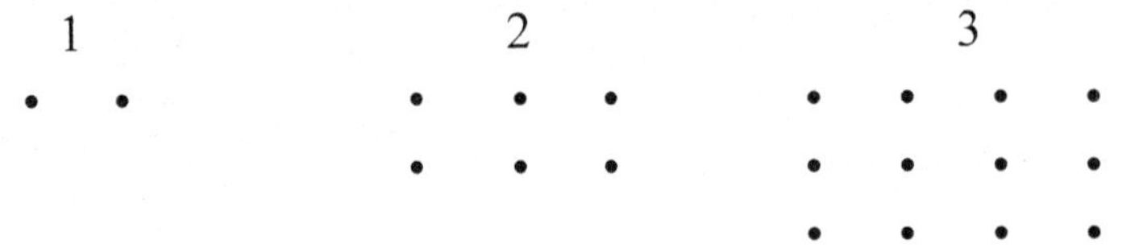

The pattern is $1 \times 1 + 1, 2 \times 2 + 2, 3 \times 3 + 3, \ldots, n \times n + n$.
The number of blocks in 10th tower is $n \times n + n = 10 \times 10 + 10 = 110$.

Problem 6. Solution: 26 (squares)
The pattern is $n + 4(n - 1)$.
$1, (1 + 1) + 2 \times 2, (1 + 1 + 1) + 2 \times 4, (1 + 1 + 1 + 1) + 2 \times 6, (1 + 1 + 1 + 1 + 1) + 2 \times 8, (1 + 1 + 1 + 1 + 1 + 1) + 2 \times 10 = 26$.

Problem 7. Solution: 211.

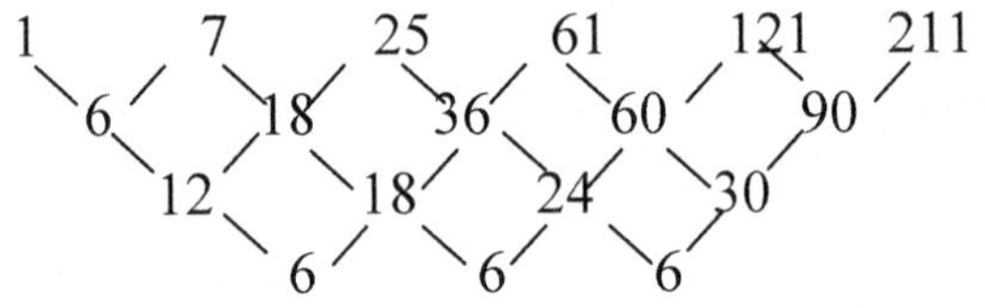

Problem 8. Solution: $\frac{9}{4}$

The pattern shows that these terms form a geometric sequence with the common ratio 2/9.

$\frac{40.5}{9} = \frac{9}{2} = \frac{2}{x} \quad \Rightarrow \quad x = \frac{9}{4}$.

Problem 9. Solution: 0.8
We change the decimal form of the numbers into fraction to observe the pattern:
$\frac{0}{1}, \frac{1}{2}, \frac{2}{3}, \frac{3}{4}, \ldots\ldots$

The next term is $\frac{4}{5}$ or 0.8.

Problem 10. Solution: *A*.

The pattern repeats every three terms.

$100 = 3 \times 33 + 1$.

So the 100th letter in the pattern is *A*.

Problem 11. Solution: *D*

We see that pattern:

$$A,$$
$$A, B,$$
$$A, B, C,$$
$$A, B, C, D,$$
$$A, B, C, D, E, \ldots$$

We know that $1 + 2 + 3 + 4 + 5 + \ldots + = \dfrac{(1+n)n}{2}$, and

$$276 = \dfrac{(1+23)\times 23}{2} < 280 < \dfrac{(1+24)\times 24}{2} = 300.$$

So 276th letter is the last letter of the 23rd row.

Thus the 277th letter is *A*. The 278th letter is *B*. The 279th letter is *C*. The 280th letter is *D*.

Problem 12. Solution: (the letter) T.

We see that pattern:

Row 1   A

Row 2   BB

Row 3   CCC

Row 4   DDDD

....

We know that $1 + 2 + 3 + 4 + 5 + \ldots + = \dfrac{(1+n)n}{2}$, and

$$190 = \dfrac{(1+19)\times 19}{2} < 200 < \dfrac{(1+20)\times 20}{2} = 210.$$

So 190th letter is the last letter of the row 19.
Thus the row 20 contains 20 T's. The 191 to 210th letters are all T's.

191st letter is A. The 278th letter is B. The 279th letter is C. The 280th letter is D.

Problem 13. Solution: 98.
The pattern is that it repeats every 10 digits: 9876543210.
9876543210 9876543210 9876543210 9876543210 9876543210 9876543210
741   852   9630   741   852   9630

So we get 6 groups of 7418529630 with six more digits of 741852.
741 852 9630 741   852 9630 741 852   9630 741 852 9630
1   2   3   4   5   6   7   8   9   0   1   2   3

We see that the pattern repeats every 3 groups. With 6 groups and six more digits
of 741852 we get 1234567890   1234567890   12
        $\Rightarrow$ 36925812 $\Rightarrow$ 98.

Problem 14. Solution: 5.
$\dfrac{1}{7} = 0.\overline{142857}$. The pattern repeats every 6 digits.
$1997 = 332 \times 6 + 5$.
Thus the 1997th digit is the same as the 5th digit, which is 5.

Problem 15. Solution: 0
$\dfrac{3}{37} = 0.\overline{081}$. The pattern repeats every 3 digits.
$199 = 66 \times 3 + 1$.
Thus the 199th digit is the same as the 1st digit, which is 0.

Problem 16. Solution: 2

$\frac{4}{7} = 0.\overline{571428}$. The pattern repeats every 6 digits.

$125 = 20 \times 6 + 5$.

Thus the 125th digit is the same as the 5th digit, which is 2.

Problem 17. Solution: (column) A

We see a pattern for every 8 integers in the table. $1599 = 1 + (n-1)2$. $n = 800$. So 1599 is the 800th number. $800 = 8 \times 9 + 8$. This means that 1959 is in the same column as the 8th number (which is 15) in the pattern. The answer is A.

Problem 18. Solution: 4th column.

We know that 1992 is even and it is either in column 2 or column 4.

We now examine the numbers in columns 1 and 4.

We see that 4th, 7th, 10th, 13th,… multiple of 3 will be in either columns 1 or 4.

We now check if $1992/3 = 664$th multiple of 3 will be in this sequence or not.

$664 = 4 + (n-1) \times 3$. n is an integer and $n = 221$. So the 664th number is indeed in this sequence. So 1992 must be in eight columns 1 or 4. We know that 1992 is even and it can only be in column 4.

Problem 19. Solution: 761.

 We turn the number arrangement the following way. We are looking at a number directly above the number 723.

Row 1	1				
Row 2	2	3			
Row 3	4	5	6		
Row 4	7	8	9	10	
Row 5	11	12	13	14	15

…

$1 + 2 + 3 + … + n = \dfrac{n(n+1)}{2}$.

We know that $\dfrac{37(37+1)}{2} = 703 < 723 < \dfrac{38(38+1)}{2} = 741$.

So the first number in the 38th row is 704 and 704 + 19 = 723. 741 is the last number in row 38.

So the first number in the 39th row is 742 and 742 + 19 = 761. So 761 is the number directly above 723.

Problem 20. Solution: 144.

We are looking for a pattern:

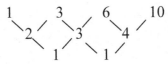

By the Newton's Little Formula

$$a_n = 1\binom{n-1}{0} + 2\binom{n-1}{1} + 1\binom{n-1}{2} = 1 + 2(n-1) + \frac{(n-1)(n-2)}{2} = \frac{(n+1)n}{2}$$

$$\frac{n(n+1)}{2} - \frac{(n-1)n}{2} = 12 \qquad \Rightarrow \qquad n = 12.$$

$$\frac{n(n+1)}{2} + \frac{(n-1)n}{2} = \frac{12(12+1)}{2} + \frac{(12-1)12}{2} = 144.$$

Problem 21. Solution: 32 (units)

We are looking for a pattern:

$1 \times 4, \quad 2 \times 4, \quad 3 \times 4, \dots 8 \times 4 = 32.$

Problem 22. Solution: (stage) 9

Stage	Fractional part
1	1/4
2	$1/4 + 3 \times (1/4)^2$.
3	$1/4 + 3 \times (1/4)^2 + 3^2 \times (1/4)^3$
4	$1/4 + 3 \times (1/4)^2 + 3^2 \times (1/4)^3 + 3^3 \times (1/4)^4$

This is a geometric sequence with the common ratio 3/4.

$$S_n = \frac{a_1(1-q^n)}{1-q} .$$

$$S_8 = \frac{\frac{1}{4} \times [1 - (\frac{3}{4})^8]}{1 - \frac{3}{4}} = 0.899887$$

$$S_9 = \frac{\frac{1}{4} \times [1 - (\frac{3}{4})^9]}{1 - \frac{3}{4}} = 0.924915$$

The answer is 9.

Problem 23. Solution: (D):

Step	Number of triangles	Number of shaded triangles
1	1	0
2	4	$0 + 1 = 1$
3	9	$1 + 2 = 3$
4	16	$1 + 2 + 3 = 6$
5	25	$1 + 2 + 3 + 4 = 10$
6	36	$1 + 2 + 3 + 4 + 5 = 15$
7	49	$1 + 2 + 3 + 4 + 5 + 6 = 21$
8	64	$1 + 2 + 3 + 4 + 5 + 6 + 7 = 28$
9	81	$1 + 2 + 3 + 4 + 5 + 6 + 7 + 8 = 36$

The ratio at step eight: $36/81 = 4/9$.

Problem 24. Solution: $\dfrac{3^9}{2^{18}}$

1	1
2	$\dfrac{3}{2^2}$
3	$\dfrac{3^2}{2^4}$
4	$\dfrac{3^3}{2^6}$
…	…

10          $\dfrac{3^9}{2^{18}}$.

Problem 25. Solution: $\dfrac{85}{256}$.

$1/4 + 1 \times (1/4)^2 + 1 \times (1/4)^3 + 1 \times (1/4)^4 = \dfrac{85}{256}$.

Problem 26. Solution: 15

$\dfrac{n(n+1)}{2} = 120 \qquad \Rightarrow \qquad n(n+1) = 240 = 15 \times 16 \qquad \Rightarrow \qquad n = 15.$

Problem 27. Solution: 170.5 (square units).

Step   square units
Change 1   128
2   128 + 32
3   128 + 32 + 8
4   128 + 32 + 8 + 2
5   128 + 32 + 8 + 2 + 0.5 = 170.5.
The answer is 170.5 (square units).

Problem 28. Solution: 76
The pattern is $n \times 2 + (n-2) \times 2$ or $n^2 - (n-2)^2$.
$20 \times 2 + (20 - 2) \times 2 = 40 + 36 = 76.$

BASIC KNOWLEDGE REVIEW

Statements

A statement is any sentence that is either true or false, but not both.

Examples:

Boston is a city in USA.

$1 + 1 = 3$

A spider does not have six legs.

The following sentences are not statements:

Do your homework.	(a command)
How do you solve this math problem?	(a question)
SAT test is harder than ACT test.	(an opinion)
This sentence is false.	(a paradox)

Negations

The sentence "SAT math test consists of 54 problems" is a statement; the negation of this statement is "SAT math test does not consists of 54 problems". The negation of a true statement is false, and the negation of a false statement is true.

Statement	Negation
All do	Some do not (Not all do)
Some do	None do (All do not)

Examples: Form the negation of each statement:

The moon is not a star.	$\Rightarrow$	The moon is a star.
The moon is a star.	$\Rightarrow$	The moon is not a star.
A spider does not have six legs.	$\Rightarrow$	A spider has six legs.

Some rabbits have short tails.	⟹ No rabbit has a short tail.
Some rabbits do not have short tails. ⟹	All rabbits have short tails.
No rabbit has a short tail.	⟹ Some rabbits have short tails.

Converse, Inverse, and Contrapositive

Direct statement	If p, then q.
Converse	If q, then p.
Inverse	If not p, then not q.
Contrapositive	If not q, then not p.

Direct statement	If I live in Boston, then I live in USA.
Converse	If I live in USA, then I live in Boston.
Inverse	If I do not live in Boston, then I do not live in USA.
Contrapositive	If I do not live in USA, then I do not live in Boston.

Rectangle of logical equivalent

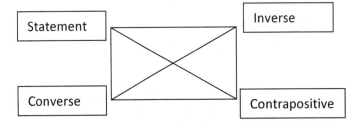

Logically equivalent pair of statements (diagonally opposite):
    A statement and its contrapositive
    The inverse and converse of the same statement

Not logically equivalent pair of statements (adjacent):
    A statement and its inverse
    A statement and its converse

The converse and contrapositive of the same statement
The inverse and contrapositive of the same statement

Examples:

Statement:	A square is a rectangle	(true)
Converse	A rectangle is a square	(false)
Inverse	A figure that is not a square is not a rectangle	(false)
Contrapositive	A figure that is not a rectangle s is not a square	(true)

Euler Diagram

Deductive reasoning consists of three steps as follows:

(1). Making a general statement (major premise).
(2). Making a particular statement (minor premise).
(3). Making a deduction (conclusion).

Example:

(1). The major premise is: All cats are animals
(2). The minor premise is: Jerry is a cat.
(3). The conclusion is: Jerry is an animal.

Procedures to draw the diagram:

(1) Draw a big circle to represent the first premise. This is the region for "animals".
(2) Draw a second circle to represent "all cats". Since all cats are animals, the second circle goes inside the first big circle.
(3) Put Jerry inside where it belongs. The second premise stated that Jerry is a cat. Put Jerry inside the region marked "Cats".

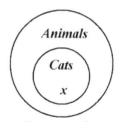

x represents Jerry

Example: Is the following argument valid? An argument is valid if that the premises are true and these premises force the conclusion to be true.

All apple trees have green leaves
That plant has green leaves.
That plant is an apple tree.

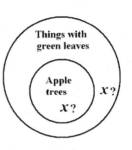

Solution: we draw the Euler Diagram. We see that "that plant" can go either inside the small circle or outside it. So the argument is not valid.

PROBLEM SOLVING SKILLS

(1). Find The Correct Order By Switching Positions

Example 1. Alexis, Britt, Carol, Danielle and Elizabeth are waiting in line. Alex is behind Carol but ahead of Danielle. Elizabeth is ahead of Britt, but behind Carol. Danielle is ahead of Britt. Who is first in line?

Solution: Carol is first in line.

We put them in an order like this:

    A   B   C   D   E.

Since Alex is behind Carol but ahead of Danielle, we order this way:

    A......B   C   D   E.
         B   C   A   D   E.

Since Elizabeth is ahead of Britt, but behind Carol, we just their position like this:

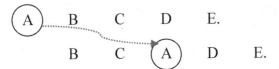

We check that it is true that Danielle is ahead of Britt.

We check that it is true that Danielle is ahead of Britt. So the correct order will be like this:

        C   A   D   E   B

Thus Carol is first in line.

(2). Find The Contrapositive Of The Statement

Example 2. Each card has either a circle or a star on one side and either a triangle or a square on the other side. In order to verify the statement "every card with a star on it also has a triangle on it," which numbered card(s) must be turned over?

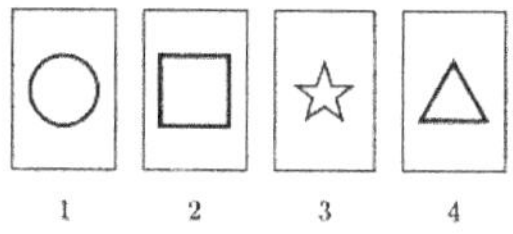

Solution: two cards (cards 2 and 3).
We introduce in this section a two-step method. This method can be used to solve any similar problems.

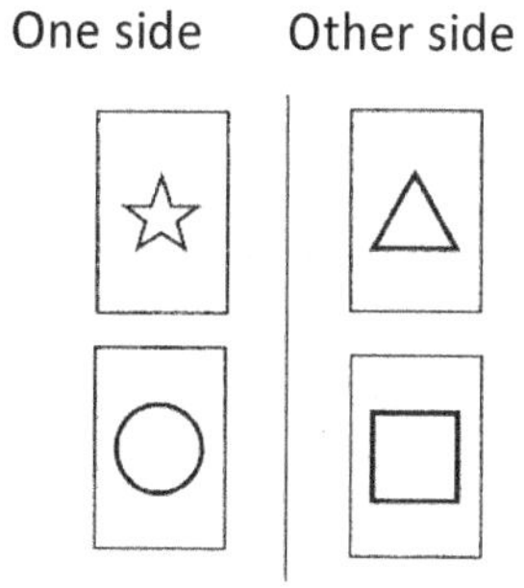

Step 1. We verify the statement first:

Every card with a star on it also has a triangle on it.

We must turn over every card with a star on it (card 3) to make sure it has a triangle on the other side.

Step 2. We then verify the contrapositive of the statement:

   Every card without a triangle on it also does not have a star on it.

We must turn over any card without a triangle on it (in this case, card 2 with a square as shown in the figure on the left) to make sure it doesn't have a star on the other side).

(3). Find Two Statements That Are Contradicted To Each Other

Example 3. There are three boxes with different colors: red, yellow and blue. One apple is in one of the three boxes. Only one of the following statements is true, and the others are false.

I: Apple is in the red box; II Apple is not in the yellow box, and III: Apple is not in the red box.

Which box is the apple in?

Solution: The apple is in the yellow box.

First we find the two statements that are contradicted to each other. There must be a true statement between these two. Other statements left are all false.

Statement I and Statement III are two contradicted statements. We are sure that the true statement is one of these two statements, although we do know which one. So we conclude that the statement II is false. Then we know the apple is in the yellow box.

(4). Find Two Statements That Are In Agreement With Each Other

Example 4. Each of three marbles A, B, and C, is colored one of the three colors. One of the marbles is colored white, one is colored red, and one is colored blue. Exactly one of these statements is true:
          1) A is red.   2) B is not blue.   3) C is not red.
What color is marble B?

Solution: B is while.
          If 1) is true, then 3) will also be true. So these two statements are in agreement with each other. However, we know that there is only one statement is true, so it must be 2). Then we know that C is red. A is not red and B is not blue. Therefore, B is white while A is blue.

(5). Focus On The Step Before The Last

Example 5. A turtle crawls up a 12 foot hill after a heavy rainstorm. The turtle crawls 4 feet, but when it stops to rest, it slides back 3 feet. How many tries does the turtle make before it makes it up the hill?

Solution: 9.

> We look at where the turtle was just before the last try. Since the turtle can crawl 4 feet each time, $12 - 4 = 8$. Every try the turtle goes up 1 foot. It takes the turtle 8 tries when it reaches the 8 feet location. The turtle needs one more try to reach the top. Note when it reaches the top, there is no sliding back.

(6). Dividing Into Three Groups

> When you need to weigh a number of coins with counterfeit coin, divide the coins into three groups with the number of coins in each group: m, m, m, or m, m, $m - 1$ or m, m, $m + 1$.

Example 6. A jeweler has four small bars that are supposed to be gold. He knows that one is counterfeit and the other three are genuine. The counterfeit bar has a slightly different weight than a real gold bar. Using a balance scale, what is the minimum number of weighings necessary to guarantee that the counterfeit bar will be detected?

Solution: 2.

We divide the four bars into three groups: 1, 1, and 2. We weight two bars, say, bar A and bar B, first.

Case I: If their weights are different, we remove one, say, bar A, and put a third bar, say bar C. If B and C are the same, and then bar A is the counterfeit. If bar B and bar C are different, bar B is the counterfeit (since it's weight is different from both A and C).

Case II: If their weights are the same, then we remove one, say, Bar A, and put a third bar, say Bar C. If B and C are the same, then Bar D is the counterfeit. If Bar B and Bar C are different, Bar C is the counterfeit.

So two weighings are necessary.

(7). Drawing Solid and Dash Lines

Example 7. Three friends – math teacher Mr. White, science teacher Mr. Black, and history teacher Mr. Redhead – met in a cafeteria. "It is interesting that one of us has white hair, another one has black hair, and the third has red hair, though no one's name gives the color of their hair" said the black-haired person. "You are right," answered White. What color is the history teacher's hair?

Solution: The history teacher's hair is black. If the relationship of two things is certain (or yes), we draw a solid line between them. Otherwise, we draw a dash line.

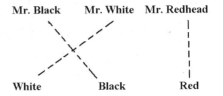

We know that no one's name gives the color of their hair. So we draw the dash lines as shown on the right:

We know that Mr. White answered the black-haired person. So he has no black hair. We draw a dash line between Mr. White and "black hair".

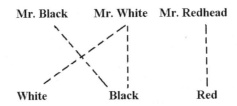

So Mr. White must have red hair. We draw a solid line to indicate that Mr. White has red hair.

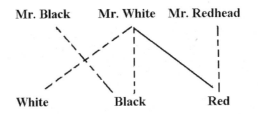

Mr. Black cannot have black hair, so he must have white hair. We draw a solid line for that.

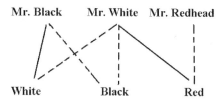

We know for sure that the history teacher's hair is black.

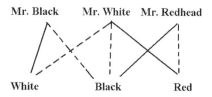

(8). Back one step and forward two

Example 8. There's a box of three hats: one black and two white. Andy and Betsy (each very smart and very logical) each place a hat on his or her head, while blindfolded. One by one, each child removes his blindfold and (without using a mirror) gets one opportunity to guess the color of the hat on his own head. If any of the two guesses correctly, everyone gets to go to the park!

First, Betsy removes her blindfold. She sees the hats that Andy is wearing, but admits that she is unable to discern her own hat color.

Then Andy says: "I can answer with my blindfold on! I know what color hat I am wearing." What color is Andy's hat?

Solution: White.
Since there is only one black hat, If Andy wears the black hat, Betsy can know immediately that she has the white hat. Now Betsy admits that she is unable to discern her own hat color. So Andy knows that his hat is white.

Example 9. There's a box of five hats: two black and three white. Andy, Betsy, and Charles (each very smart and very logical) each place a hat on his or her head, while blindfolded. One by one, each child removes his blindfold and (without using a mirror) gets one opportunity to guess the color of the hat on his own head. If any of the three guesses correctly, everyone gets to go to the park!

First, Charles removes his blindfold. He sees the hats that the others are wearing, but admits that he is unable to discern his own hat color.

Next, Betsy removes her blindfold, and sadly reveals that she too is not able to determine the color of her own hat.

Finally, Andy pipes up and says "I can answer with my blindfold on! I know what color hat I am wearing." What color is Andy's hat?

Solution: White.
We consider the case with two people, one black and two white hats. Since there is only one black hat, If Andy wears the black hat, Betsy can know immediately that she has the white hat. Now Betsy admits that she is unable to discern her own hat color. So Andy knows that his hat is white.

Now we consider three people with two black hats and three white hats.

If Andy wears black hat, for Betsy and Charles, it will be the case with two people, one black hat. So Betsy and Charles will know the answer. Since Betsy and Charles do not know the answer, so the color of Andy's hat must be white.

(9). Squeezing method

Example 10. (2014 Mathcounts National) Larry tells Mary and Jerry that he is thinking of two consecutive integers from 1 to 10. He tells Mary one of the numbers, and he tells Jerry the other number. Then the following conversation occurs between Mary and Jerry:
Mary: I don't know your number.
Jerry: I don't know your number, either.

Mary: Ah, now I know your number.

Assuming both Mary and Jerry used correct logic, what is the sum of the possible numbers Mary could have?

Solution: 22.

We list 10 numbers: 1   2   3   4   5   6   7   8   9   10.

If Mary gets 1 or 10, she will know Jerry's number (2 or 9). So her number is neither 1 nor 10.

So all the possible numbers for Mary are:

            2   3   4   5   6   7   8   9

Jerry knows that Mary's number is neither 1 nor 10. But he still cannot tell Mary's number. So his number is neither 2 nor 9. (If his number is 2, he will know that Mary's number is not 1, so Mary's number must be 3 since Mary's number and Jerry's number are consecutive integers. Same reasoning is true if his number is 9). Certainly his number is neither 1 nor 10.

If Mary's number is 2 or 9, she will be able to tell Jerry's number (3 or 9).

If Mary's number is 3 or 8, she will also be able to tell Jerry's number (4 or 7).

If Mary's number is 4, she will not be able to tell Jerry's number because Jerry's number could be either 3 or 5. Same reasoning is true if her number is 5, 6, or 7.

The sum of Mary's number is $(2 + 9) + (3 + 8) = 22$.

MORE EXAMPLES

Example 11. Squares are faster than circles, hexagons are slower than triangles, and hexagons are faster than squares. Which of these shapes is the slowest?

(A) Squares   (B) Circles   (C) Hexagons   (D) Triangles   (E) None of them

Solution: Circles.

We put them in any order as shown in the figure below:

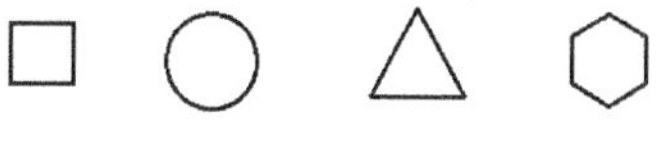

Squares are faster than circles, hexagons are slower than triangles. So we do not need to switch any order yet.

Since hexagons are faster than squares, we move the hexagon to the front. Since it is slower than triangles, we move both of them with their relative positions unchanged:

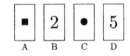

So the circles are the slowest.

Example 12. Four cards are constructed so that there is either a circle or a square on one side and an odd or even number on the other side. The cards are placed on a table as shown. Which cards must be turned to prove the following: Every square has an even number on the other side?

■	2	●	5
A	B	C	D

Solution: A and D.
We verify the statement first:
Every square has an even number on the other side
We must turn over every card with a square (card A).

We then verify the contrapositive of the statement:
Every card does not have an even number on one side does not have a square on the other side.
We must turn over any card with an odd number (card D) to make sure it doesn't have a square on the other side).
Cards A and D must be turned to prove the statement.

Example 13. Classroom window was broken. The principal had four students in his office. He knew that one of them did it, and he also knew that only one of the students told the truth, but not sure which one.
Alex said: Bob did;

Bob said: Dean did;

Cam said: not me;

Dean said: Bob lied.

Who broke the window?

Solution: Cam.

First we find which two statements contradiction: Bob and Dean. Then we know that both Alex and Cam did not tell the truth. Then we conclude that Cam did it. And only Dean told the truth.

Example 14. A sealed envelope contains a card with a single digit on it. Three of the following statements are true, and the other is false.

I. The digit is 1.

II. The digit is not 2.

III. The digit is 3.

IV. The digit is not 4.

Which one of the following must necessarily be correct?

(A) I is true.   (B) I is false.   (C) II is true.   (D) III is true. (E) IV is false

Solution: (C).

Method 1: We first find two statements that are in agreement with each other. In our case, II, and IV are not contradicting to each other. So we know that either I or III is the false statement. Thus II and IV must be true. From five choices, we see that (C) is correct answer.

We first find two statements that are contradicted to each other. In our case, I and III. So we know that either I or III is the false statement. Thus II and IV must be true. From the five choices, we see that (C) is correct answer.

Method 2: We first find two statements that are contradicted to each other. In our case, I and III. So we know that either I or III is the false statement. Thus II and IV must be true. From the five choices, we see that (C) is correct answer.

Example 15. A centipede climbs a 40-foot tree. Each day he climbs 5 feet, and each night he slides down 3 feet. In how many days will the centipede reach the top of the tree?

(A) 19   (B) 18   (C) 17   (D) 20   (E) 21

Solution: 19 days.

We look at where the centipede was just before the last climbing. Since the centipede can climb 5 feet each time, $40 - 5 = 35$. Every time the centipede goes up $5 - 3 = 2$ feet. The greatest height the centipede can go before he reaches the top is 36 feet. When the centipede reaches 36 high, he has spending $36 \div 2 = 18$ days. The centipede needs one more day to reach the top. Note when it reaches the top, there is no sliding back.

Example 16. Alex has 6 coins. Five of the 6 coins weigh the same and one coin is heavier. If Alex had a balance scale, what is the least number of times he could weigh coins to be sure he could determine which coin was heavier?

Solution: 2.

Method 1: Divide the 6 coins into two groups. Each group has 3 coins. Put each group on each side of the balance scale. One side would be heavier. Taking those coins, put one on each side of the balance scale. If it balances, then the one off the scale is heavier. If it does not balance, you will know which one is heavier.
Method 2: Divide 6 coins into three groups. Each group has two coins. Taking two groups, put each group on each side of the balance scale. If it balances, then the group off the scale contains the heavier coin. The second weighing will tell which coin is heavier. If it does not balance, you take the coins from the heavier side and weight one more time to know which one is heavier.

Example 17. In a horse race game on a computer, Secretariat, Man-Of-War, Affirmed and Citation finished in first through fourth places (not necessarily in that order), with no ties. Man-Of-War finished second or fourth. Affirmed did not win the race. Citation or Secretariat finished third. Man-Of-War beat Secretariat. What is the name of the horse that finished fourth?

Solution: A.

Method 1. This method is also good for more complicated logic reasoning problems.

Since Affirmed did not win, we can draw a dash line between A and 1.

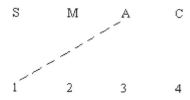

Since M finished second or fourth, then M did not finish 1 or 3. We draw a dash line between M and 1 and a dash line between M and 3.

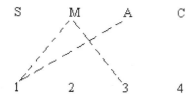

Since S was beaten by M, so S was not the first. We draw a dash line between S and 1.

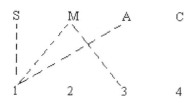

At the moment, we know that C finished first. So we draw a solid line between C and 1.

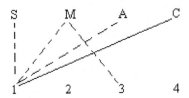

Since C or S finished third, and we know that C is not third, S must be third. We draw a solid line between S and 3.

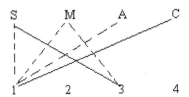

Since M beat S. M must be second. We draw a solid line between M and 2.

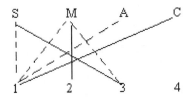

The only place left for A is the fourth. So we conclude that **A finished fourth**.

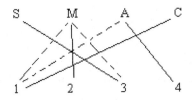

Method 2:

M is 2nd or 4th. Since M beat S, so M can't be 4th and M should be 2nd. Third place has been taken by S or C, so A could not be 3rd, and A did not win, so A must be 4th.

Example 18. Below are the four labeled boxes. Each box is painted a different color. There is a red box, which is next to a blue box. There is a green box, which is next to the red box and a yellow box. Which box could be painted red?

$\boxed{1}\ \boxed{2}\ \boxed{3}\ \boxed{4}$

(A) 1 only   (B) 2 only   (C) 3 only   (D) 2 or 3   (E) 1 or 4

Solution: D.
There is a red box, which is next to a blue box.
So we have two cases:
R   B
B   R

There is a green box, which is next to the red box and a yellow box.
So we also have two cases:
Y   G   R
R   G   Y

Therefore we can have two cases:
1   2   3   4
Y   G   R   B
B   R   G   Y
Therefore, either box 2 or box 3 could be painted red.

☆**Example 19.** (AMC 8) Amy, Bill and Celine are friends with different ages. Exactly one of the following statements is true.
I. Bill is the oldest.
II. Amy is not the oldest.
III. Celine is not the youngest.
Rank the friends from the oldest to the youngest.
(A) Bill, Amy, Celine   (B) Amy, Bill, Celine   (C) Celine, Amy, Bill
(D) Celine, Bill, Amy   (E) Amy, Celine, Bill

Solution (our solution): (E).

We find two statements that are in agreement: I and II. We know that exactly one of the three statements is true. So III is true and I and II are false. Celine is not the youngest. Amy is the oldest and Bill is the youngest.
The correct order from oldest to youngest is Amy, Celine, Bill.

☆**Example 20.** (AMC 8) Five friends compete in a dart-throwing contest. Each one has two darts to throw at the same circular target, and each individual's score is the sum of the scores in the target regions that are hit. The scores for the target regions are the whole numbers 1 through 10. Each throw hits the target in a region with a different value. The scores are: Alice 16 points, Ben 4 points, Cindy 7 points, Dave 11 points, and Ellen 17 points. Who hits the region worth 6 points?
(A) Alice   (B) Ben   (C) Cindy   (D) Dave   (E) Ellen

Solution: (A).
Method 1: Ben must hit 1 and 3. This means Cindy must hit 5 and 2, because she scores 7 using two different numbers, neither of which is 1 or 3. By similar reasoning, Alice hits 10 and 6, Dave hits 7 and 4, and Ellen hits 9 and 8. Alice hits the 6.

Method 2:
Ellen's score can be obtained by either $10 + 7$ or $9 + 8$. In the first case, it is impossible for Alice to score 16. So Ellen's 17 is obtained by scoring 9 and 8, and Alice's total of 16 is the result of her hitting 10 and 6. The others scored $11 = 7 + 4$, $7 = 5 + 2$ and $4 = 3 + 1$.

PROBLEMS

Problem 1. There are 9 apparently identical balls, except that one is heavier than the other 8. What is the smallest number of balance scale weighings required to ensure identification of the "odd" ball?
(A) 9   (B) 3   (C) 4   (D) 1   (E) 2

Problem 2. A kitchen pantry has five shelves, each containing a specific kind of food. The spices are on the shelf directly below the vegetables, the fruits are above the bread, and the vegetables are 3 shelves below the cereals. Which kind of food is on the third shelf?
(A) vegetables   (B) fruits   (C) bread   (D) cereals   (E) spices

Problem 3. At Hope Middle School, Mr. Eye, Mr. Love and Mr. Problems teach science, mathematics, and history—but not necessarily in that order. The history teacher, who was an only child, has the least experience. Mr. Problems, who married Mr. Eye's sister, has more experience than the science teacher. Who teaches science?

Problem 4. Five coins look the same, but one is a counterfeit coin with a different weight than each of the four genuine coins. Using a balance scale, what is the least number of weighings needed to ensure that, in every case, the counterfeit coin is found and is shown to be heavier or lighter?
(A) 5   (B) 4   (C) 3   (D) 2   (E) 1

Problem 5. A centipede climbs a 40-foot tree. Each day he climbs 5 feet, and each night he slides down 2 feet. In how many days will the centipede reach the top of the tree?
(A) 14   (B) 13   (C) 12   (D) 8   (E) 20

Problem 6. Adam, Ben, Charles, David and Ed were waiting in line. Adam is between Ben and Chase. Ben is between David and Adam. Ed is also between David and Adam. Ben is between David and Ed. Who is in the middle of the line?

(A) Adam   (B) Ben   (C) Charles   (D) David   (E) Ed

Problem 7. Five cards are lying on a table as shown. Each card has a letter on one side and a whole number on the other side. Jane said, "If a vowel is on one side of any card, then an even number is on the other side." Mary showed Jane was wrong by turning over one card. Which card did Mary turn over?

$\boxed{3}$ $\boxed{4}$ $\boxed{6}$ $\boxed{P}$ $\boxed{Q}$

(A) 5   (B) 4   (C) 3   (D) 2   (E) 1

Problem 8. A centipede crawl a tree 75-inches high, starting from the ground. Each day it crawls 5 inches, and each night it slides down 4 inches. When will it first reach the top of the tree?
(A) 15   (B) 18   (C) 19   (D) 72   (E) 71.

Problem 9. There are 4 cards on the table with the symbols a, b, 4, and 5 written on their visible sides. What is the smallest number of cards we need to turn over to find out whether the following statement is true: "If an even number is written on one side of a card then a vowel is written on the other side?

Problem 10. Each of the cards shown below has a number on one side and a letter on the other. How many of the cards must be turned over to prove the correctness of the statement: Every card with a vowel on one side has a prime number on the other side.

$\boxed{A}$ $\boxed{B}$ $\boxed{E}$ $\boxed{4}$ $\boxed{5}$ $\boxed{6}$ $\boxed{8}$

(A) 7   (B) 6   (C) 5   (D) 4   (E) 3

Problem 11. Three kids are playing pitcher, catcher and infielder. Sam is not the catcher. The infielder lives next to Sam. The catcher and John go to the same school. What position does Alex play?

Problem 12. Cookies were missing, taken by either Alex, Bob, or Charles. Each person said:

Alex: I did not take the cookies.
Bob: Charles took the cookies.
Charles: That is true

If at least one of them lied and at least one told the truth, who took the cookies?

Problem 13. Each of the cards shown has a number on one side and a letter on the other. How many of the cards must be turned over to prove the correctness of this statement for these cards: "If a card has a vowel on one side, then it has a prime number on the other side?"

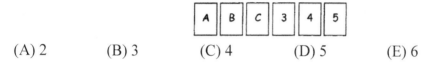

(A) 2   (B) 3   (C) 4   (D) 5   (E) 6

Problem 14. If all alligators are ferocious creatures and some creepy crawlers are alligators, which statement(s) must be true?

I. All alligators are creepy crawlers.
II. Some ferocious creatures are creepy crawlers.
III. Some alligators are not creepy crawlers.

(A) I only   (B) II only   (C) III only   (D) II and III only
(E) None must be true

Problem 15. A number of bacteria are placed in a container. One second later each bacterium divides into two, the next second each of the resulting bacteria divided in two again, et al. After one minute the container is full. When was the container half full?
(A) 58   (B) 59   (C) 60   (D) 120   (E) 119

Problem 16. If the two statements below are true, which of the following statements must also be true?
(1) Alex sometimes goes to adventure movies.

(2) Betsy never goes to comedy movies.

I. Alex never goes to comedy movies.
II. Betsy sometimes goes to adventure movies.
III. Alex and Betsy never go to comedy movies together.

(A) I only   (B) II only   (C) III only   (D) I and III   (E) II and III

Problem 17. The four children in the Jones family are Alex, Bob, Cathy, and Debra. Bob is neither the youngest nor the oldest. Debra is one of the two younger children. Cathy is the oldest child. Alex is often taking care of his younger brother and sister. Who is the youngest child?

(A) Bob   (B) Debra   (C) Alex   (D) Cathy
(E) It cannot be determined from the information

Problem 18. Sam is not a member of the math club, then from which of the following statements can it be determined whether or not Sam is in the science club?

(A) Anyone in the math club is not in the science club.
(B) No one is in both the math club and the science club.
(C) Anyone who is not in the math club is not in the science club.
(D) Everyone in the math club is in the science club.
(E) Some people who are not in the math club are not in the science club.

Problem 19. If the statement "If a number is in list A, it is not in list B" is true, which of the following statements must also be true?
(A) If a number is not in list A, it is in list B.
(B) If a number is not in list B, it is in list A.
(C) If a number is in list B, it is not in list A.
(D) If a number is in list B, it is in list A.
(E) If a number is in list A, it is also in list B.

Problem 20. The Hope Middle School has three clubs: math, reading, and writing. Five students from a family each participated in one club only. The statements below are about what these five students participated. If n is the number of students who participated in the reading club, which of the following statements is true?
The first student participated in the math club.
The second student did not participate in the math club.
The third student participated in the reading club.
The fourth student participated in the same club as the first student.
The fifth student participated in the same club as the second student.
(A) n must be 1.   (B) n must be 2.   (C) n must be 3.   (D) n must be 1 or 2.
(E) n must be 1 or 3.

Problem 21. If the statement "Some integers in set X are odd" is true, which of the following must also be true?

(A) If an integer is odd, it is in set X.   (B) If an integer is even, it is in set X.
(C) All integers in set X are odd.   (D) All integers in set X are even.
(E) Not all integers in set X are even.

Problem 22. If all boys in the math club are good at math. Which of the following statements must be true?
(A) No boy whose math is not good is a member of the math club.
(B) All boys whose math is good are members of the math club.
(C) All boys who are not members of the math are not good at math.
(D) Every member of the math club whose math is good is a boy.
(E) There is one boy in the math club whose math is not good.

Problem 23. At Hope High School, some members of the math club are on the science team and no members of the science team are 9th graders. Which of the following must also be true?

(A) No members of the math club are 9th graders.
(B) Some members of the math club are 9th graders.

(C) Some member of the math club are not 9th graders.

(D) More 9th graders are on the science team than are in the math club.

(E) More 9th graders are in the math club than are on the science team.

Problem 24. The teacher whispers positive integer A to Anna, B to Brett, and C to Chris. The students don't know one another's numbers but they do know that the sum of their numbers is 14. Anna says, "I know that Brett and Chris have different numbers". Then Brett says, "I already knew that all three of our numbers were different". Finally, Chris announces, "Now I know all three of our numbers". What is the product ABC? (Mathcounts)

SOLUTIONS

Problem 1. Solution: 2.
We divide the 9 balls into three groups: 3, 3, and 3. We weight two groups, say, group A and group B, first.

Case I: If their weights are different, let us say, group A is heavier. We know that group A contains the odd ball. We divide three balls into 1, 1, and 1. We weight two of them. If these two are the same weight, then the one left is the odd ball. If these two have the different weights, the heavier one is the odd ball. So we need two weighings.

Case II: If their weights are the same, then we the group C contains the odd ball. We then follow the procedure in Case I. So we need two weighings.

Therefore two weighings are necessary.

Problem 2. Solution: Bread.
We place them in any order like the following:
spices vegetables,   fruits   bread,   cereals.

Since spices are on the shelf directly below the vegetables, we switch the position of them as follows:
vegetables   spices   fruits   bread   cereals

Since the fruits are above the bread, we do not change their positions.
Since the vegetables are 3 shelves below the cereals, we move cereals to the top and switch the positions of fruits and bread as follows:
cereals   fruits   bread vegetables   spices
We are done and we know that bread is on the third shelf.

Problem 3. Solution: Mr. Eye.
We know that Mr. Problems, who married Mr. Eye's sister, has more experience than the science teacher, and the history teacher, who was an only child, has the

least experience. So we are sure that Mr. Problems is neither science teacher and nor history teacher. He must be math teacher.

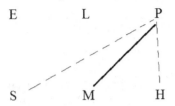

Mr. Eye is not the history teacher because he has a sister and the history teacher is the only child. So he must be the science teacher. We are done.

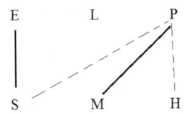

Problem 4. Solution: 3.

We divide the five coins into A, B, and C three groups: 2 (coins a and b), 2 (coins c and d), and 1 (coin e). We weight groups A and B.

Case I: If they weigh the same, coin e is the counterfeit coin. In this case, one weighing is needed.

Case II: If their weights are different, we remove one group, say, group A, and weigh the two coins c and d.

If coins c and d have the same weight, then we know that one of the coins (either a or b is the counterfeit coin. Then we weigh coins a and e. If they have the same weight, coin b is the counterfeit coin. . If they have the different weight, coin a is the counterfeit coin. We need to weigh 3 times.

If coins c and d have the different weight, then we know that one of the coins (either c or d is the counterfeit coin. Then we weigh coins c and e. If they have the same weight, coin *d* is the counterfeit coin. . If they have the different weight, coin *c* is the counterfeit coin. We also need to weigh 3 times.

So the worst case is that we need 3 weighings.

Problem 5. Solution: 13 days.

We look at where the centipede was just before the last try. Since the centipede can crawl $5 - 2 = 3$ feet each day-night, $40 = 3 \times 12 + 4$. It takes the centipede 12 tries when it reaches the 36 feet location. The centipede needs one more try to reach the top. Note when it reaches the top, there is no sliding back.

Problem 6. Solution: Ed.

We place them in any order like the following:

A   B   C   D   E

Since Adam is between Ben and Chase, we switch the position of them as follows:

B   A   C   D   E

Since Ben is between David and Adam, we move D to the front as follows:

D   B   A   C   E

Since Ed is also between David and Adam, we move D to the position below:

D   B   A   C

E

Since Ben is between David and Ed, we know that the arrangement is as follows:

D   B   E   A   C

We are done and we know that Ed is in the middle of the line.

Problem 7. Solution: Card 3.

We verify the statement first:

If a vowel is on one side of any card, then an even number is on the other side.
We have zero card to turn over.
We then verify the contrapositive of the statement:
Every card does not have an even number on one side does not have a vowel on the other side.
We must turn over any card with a composite number (card 3 only) to make sure it doesn't have a vowel on the other side).

Problem 8. Solution: The caterpillar will be on the top of the tree at the end of the 71st day. We look at where the centipede was just before the last try. Since the centipede can crawl $5 - 4 = 1$ foot each day-night, $75 = 1 \times 70 + 5$. It takes the centipede 70 tries when it reaches the 70 feet location. The centipede needs one more try to reach the top. Note when it reaches the top, there is no sliding back.

Problem 9. Solution: Two cards need to be turned over (Cards "4" and "b")
We verify the statement first:
"If an even number is written on one side of a card then a vowel is written on the other side".

We must turn over every card with an even number (card 4) to make sure it has a vowel on the other side.
We then verify the contrapositive of the statement:
"If a vowel is not written on the one side of a card then an even number is not written is written on the other side".

We must turn over any card not with a vowel (card b) to make sure it doesn't have an even number on the other side).
So we need to turn over $1 + 1 = 2$ cards.

Problem 10. Solution: We must overturn five cards.
We verify the statement first:
Every card with a vowel on one side has a prime number on the other side.

We must turn over every card with a vowel (cards A and E) to make sure it has a prime on the other side.

We then verify the contrapositive of the statement:

Every card without a prime number on one side does not have a vowel on the other side.

We must turn over any card with a composite number (cards 4, 6, and 8) to make sure it doesn't have a vowel on the other side).

Problem 11. Solution: Alex plays catcher. Sam is not the catcher. Since John and the catcher go to the same school, John is not the catcher. Therefore, Alex is the catcher.

Problem 12. Solution: Bob took the cookies.
If Charles took the cookies, then all of them told the truth. If Alex took the cookies, then all of them lied. If Bob took the cookies, then Bob and Charles lied, but Alex told the truth.

Problem 13. Solution: 2 (Cards A and 4).
To verify this statement:

One side	Other side
A	3
B	4
C	5

If a card has a vowel on one side, then it has a prime number on the other side
We need to turn over any card with a vowel on it. So we need to turn over card A.
We also need to test its contrapositive:

If a card does not have a prime number on one side, then it does not have a vowel on the other side"

In this case, we need to verify any card without a prime number on it (card marked 4).

Problem 14. Solution: (B)
From the conditions we can conclude that some creepy crawlers are ferocious (since some are alligators). Hence, there are some ferocious

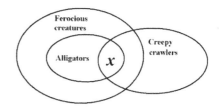

creatures that are creepy crawlers, and thus II must be true. The diagram below shows that the only conclusion that can be drawn is existence of an animal in the region with the dot. Thus, neither I nor III follows from the given conditions.

Problem 15. Solution: After 59 seconds.
We think backward and focus on the step before the last. At 59 seconds, it is half full. Then after one minute the container will be full.

Problem 16. Solution: C.
The statement "Alex sometimes goes to adventure movies" does not necessarily mean that "Alex never goes to comedy movies". So I is not necessarily correct. We can cross out (A) and (D).
For the same reason we II is not necessarily correct. We can cross out (B) and (E).
Now we can just choose the answer (C) since it is the only answer left or we can do more work as follows:
From the statement "Betsy never goes to comedy movies", we know for sure that that Alex and Betsy never go to comedy movies together. So III is correct.

Problem 17. Solution: B.
First we put them in the following order:
A   B   C   D.
Since Cathy is the oldest, we switch her position to the left most.
C   A   B   D.
Alex is often taking care his younger brother and sister so his position is okay.
Bob is neither the youngest nor the oldest so his position is also okay.
Therefore Debra is the youngest child

Problem 18. Solution: C.
(A) Anyone in the math club is not in the science club.
This one does not apply to Sam since he is not in the math club.
(B) No one is in both the math club and the science club.
This one does not apply to Sam since he is not in the math club.
(C) Anyone who is not in the math club is not in the science club.
This statement directly applies to Sam. Since he is not in the math club, he is not in the science club.

(D) Everyone in the math club is in the science club.
This one does not apply to Sam since he is not in the math club.
(E) Some people who are not in the math club are not in the science club.
"Some people" may or may not include Sam. So from this statement we are not able to determine whether or not Sam is in the science club.

Problem 19. Solution: C.
We only need to write out the contrapositive of the statement:
If a number is in list B, it is not in list A.
Which is (C).

Problem 20. Solution: E.
We list the possible outcomes:

1	2	3	4	5
Math	Not Math	Reading	Math	Same as 2

We see that
Case I: if the second student participated in reading club, so does the 5th student. In this case there will be 3 students who participated in the reading club.
Case II: if the second student participated in writing club, so does the 5th student. In this case there will be 1 student who participated in the reading club.
The answer is then (E).

Problem 21. Solution: (E).
If some integers in set are odd, then those odd integers are members of set that are not even. So not all integers in set are even.

Problem 12. Solution: A.
The contrapositive of the statement "all boys in the math club are good at math" is: "If a boy's math is not good, he is not a member of the math club".
Which is equivalent to: (A) No boy whose math is not good is a member of the math club.

Problem 23. Solution: (C). Some member of the math club are not 9th graders.

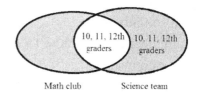

Math club   Science team

Problem 24. Solution: 42.
There are two possible ways to have a sum of 14 for three numbers:
Even, even, even; or odd, odd, even.

Since Anna says, "I know that Brett and Chris have different numbers", her number must be odd. If her number is even, let us say, 2, then other two numbers could be 6 and 6. So she will not be able to tell that that Brett and Chris have different numbers.

So we know that three numbers must be odd, odd, and even.

Brett was able to tell that all three of our numbers were different but he was not able to know all three numbers.

So Brett's number is also odd but not 1, 3, nor 5. If his number is one of them, that number may match with Anna's number.

So Brett's number must be 7, or 9, but not 11. If his number were 11, he would know all three numbers ($14 = 11 + 1 + 2$). And Anna's number must be 1, 3 or 5.

If Brett's number is 9, we have $14 - 9 = 5$. And $5 = 1 + 4 = 3 + 2$. So he cannot tell each person's numbers.

If his number is 7, we have $14 - 7 = 7$. And $7 = 5 + 2 = 3 + 4 = 1 + 6$. So he cannot tell each person's numbers.

Chris was able to tell all three numbers. His number could be 6, 4, or 2.
If his number is 2, we have $14 = 5 + 7 + 2 = 3 + 9 + 2$. So he cannot tell each person's numbers.
If his number is 4, we have $14 = 3 + 7 + 4 = 1 + 9 + 4$. So he cannot tell each person's numbers.
If his number is 6, we have $14 = 1 + 7 + 6$. So he can tell each person's numbers.
The product is $1 \times 7 \times 6 = 42$.

1.TERMS:

Fraction: A part of a whole or a quotient of two numbers, expressed as $\dfrac{a}{b}$. a and b are whole numbers. $b \neq 0$. $\dfrac{a}{b}$ is the same as $a \div b$ or a/b.

Proper fraction: A fraction in which the numerator is less than the denominator: $\dfrac{3}{5}$. Such a fraction has a value less than 1.

Improper fraction: A fraction in which the numerator is greater than or equal to the denominator: $\dfrac{5}{3}$. It has a value greater than or equal to 1.

Mixed number: A mixed number contains both a whole number part and a fraction part and can be written as an improper fraction: $2\dfrac{1}{3} = \dfrac{2 \times 3 + 1}{3} = \dfrac{7}{3}$.

2. PROPERTIES:

2.1. Equivalent Fraction (Cancellation Law): Two fractions are equal if they represent the same portion of a whole.

$$\frac{1}{2} \qquad\qquad = \qquad\qquad \frac{2}{4} \qquad\qquad = \qquad\qquad \frac{6}{12}$$

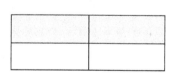

Examples: $\dfrac{38}{57} = \dfrac{2 \times 19}{3 \times 19} = \dfrac{2}{3}$; $\dfrac{38}{57} = \dfrac{38 \div 19}{57 \div 19} = \dfrac{2}{3}$

2.2. Fundamental Law of Fractions:

For any fraction $\dfrac{a}{b}$ and any number $c \neq 0$, $\dfrac{a}{b} = \dfrac{a \times c}{b \times c}$.

(The value of a fraction does not change if its numerator and denominator are multiplied by the same nonzero number).

Example. $\dfrac{2}{3} = \dfrac{2 \times 5}{3 \times 5} = \dfrac{10}{15}$.

2.3. Lowest (Reduced; Simplest) Term: A fraction in which the numerator and the denominator have no common terms except 1. The lowest terms are obtained by taking all the common factors out of the numerator and the denominator.

$\dfrac{10}{15}$ is not a fraction in the lowest term but $\dfrac{2}{3}$ is. ($\dfrac{10}{15} = \dfrac{2 \times 5}{3 \times 5} = \dfrac{2}{3}$).

2.4. Additon and Subtraction:

When working with fractions, only the numerators in fractions are added or subtracted.

(1). Two fractions having the same denominators:

We just add or subtract the numerators.

$$\dfrac{a}{b} + \dfrac{c}{b} = \dfrac{a+c}{b} \qquad \Rightarrow \qquad \dfrac{3}{5} + \dfrac{1}{5} = \dfrac{3+1}{5} = \dfrac{4}{5}$$

$$\dfrac{a}{b} - \dfrac{c}{b} = \dfrac{a-c}{b} \qquad \Rightarrow \qquad \dfrac{3}{5} - \dfrac{1}{5} = \dfrac{3-1}{5} = \dfrac{2}{5}$$

(2). Two fractions having the different denominators:

We convert them to the same denominators first, and then add the numerators.

$$\dfrac{a}{b} + \dfrac{c}{d} = \dfrac{a \times d}{b \times d} + \dfrac{c \times b}{b \times d} = \dfrac{a \times d + c \times b}{b \times d} \Rightarrow$$

$$\dfrac{1}{2} + \dfrac{2}{5} = \dfrac{1 \times 5}{2 \times 5} + \dfrac{2 \times 2}{5 \times 2} = \dfrac{5+4}{10} = \dfrac{9}{10}$$

$$\dfrac{a}{b} - \dfrac{c}{d} = \dfrac{a \times d}{b \times d} - \dfrac{c \times b}{b \times d} = \dfrac{a \times d - c \times b}{b \times d} \Rightarrow$$

$$\dfrac{1}{2} - \dfrac{2}{5} = \dfrac{1 \times 5}{2 \times 5} - \dfrac{2 \times 2}{5 \times 2} = \dfrac{5-4}{10} = \dfrac{1}{10}$$

2.5. Multiplication of Fractions

The numerator of the product is obtained by multiplying together the numerators. The denominator of the product is obtained by multiplying together the denominators.

$$\frac{a}{b} \times \frac{c}{d} = \frac{a \times c}{b \times d} \qquad \Rightarrow \qquad \frac{2}{5} \times \frac{3}{7} = \frac{2 \times 3}{5 \times 7} = \frac{6}{35}$$

2.6. Division of Fractions

To divide by a fraction, we simply multiply by its reciprocal.

$$\frac{a}{b} \div \frac{c}{d} = \frac{a}{b} \times \frac{d}{c} = \frac{ad}{bc} \qquad \Rightarrow \qquad \frac{2}{5} \div \frac{3}{7} = \frac{2}{5} \times \frac{7}{3} = \frac{2 \times 7}{5 \times 3} = \frac{14}{15}$$

The reciprocal of a number is obtained by switching the numerator and the

denominator. For example, the reciprocal of $\frac{2}{3}$ is $\frac{3}{2}$, and the reciprocal of 2 (note

that 2 can be written as $\frac{2}{1}$) is $\frac{1}{2}$.

$$\frac{\dfrac{a}{b}}{\dfrac{c}{d}} = \frac{ad}{bc}$$

3. PROBLEM SOLVING SKILLS

3.1. Comparing Fractions

(1). Same Denominator:

The fraction with a larger numerator is larger: $\frac{3}{5} > \frac{1}{5}$

(2). Same Numerator:

The fraction with a larger denominator is smaller: $\dfrac{3}{7} < \dfrac{3}{5}$

(3). Both the numerator and denominator are not the same

$3 \times 11 = 33$ $4 \times 8 = 32$

$\dfrac{3}{8}$ $\overset{2}{\diagdown\!\!\diagup}$ $\dfrac{}{11}$ $\Rightarrow$ $33 > 32$ $\Rightarrow$ $\dfrac{3}{8} > \dfrac{4}{11}$

Example 1. Mary made two pies that were exactly the same size. The first pie was a cherry pie, which she cut into 6 equal slices. The second was a pumpkin pie, which she cut into 12 equal pieces. Mary takes her pies to a party. People eat 3 slices of cherry pie and 6 slices of pumpkin pie. Did people eat more cherry pie or pumpkin pie?

Solution: People eat the same amount of cherry pie and pumpkin pie.

$\dfrac{3}{6} = \dfrac{6}{12} = \dfrac{1}{2}$. People eat the same amount of cherry pie and pumpkin pie.

Example 2. Peter has two cakes that are the same size. The first cake was chocolate, which he cut 12 equal parts. The second cake was marble, which he cut into 6 equal parts. His family eats 5 slices of chocolate cake and 3 slices of marble cake. Did they eat more chocolate cake or marble cake?

Solution: They eat more marble cake.

$\dfrac{5}{12} < \dfrac{3}{6}$. They eat more marble cake.

☆**Example 3.** (AMC 8) What is the correct ordering of the three numbers 5/19, 7/21, and 9/23, in increasing order?

(A) $\dfrac{9}{23} < \dfrac{7}{21} < \dfrac{5}{19}$ (B) $\dfrac{5}{19} < \dfrac{7}{21} < \dfrac{9}{23}$ (C) $\dfrac{9}{23} < \dfrac{5}{19} < \dfrac{7}{21}$

(D) $\dfrac{5}{19} < \dfrac{9}{23} < \dfrac{7}{21}$ (E) $\dfrac{7}{21} < \dfrac{5}{19} < \dfrac{9}{23}$

Solution: (B).
Method 1:

Using a common denominator, 5/19 = 105/399 and 7/21 = 133/399 , so 5/19 < 7/21.
Also 7/21 = 161/483 and 9/23 = 189/483, so 7/21 < 9/23 .

Method 2:
Comparing each fraction, 7/21 = 1/3 , 5/19 < 5/15 = 1/3 , and 9/23 > 9/27 = 1/3 , so the correct increasing order is 5/19 < 7/21 < 9/23 .

3.2. Sum of A Series of Fractions

Useful formulas:

$$\frac{1}{n(n+1)} = \frac{1}{n} - \frac{1}{n+1} \qquad \Rightarrow \qquad \frac{1}{3(3+1)} = \frac{1}{3} - \frac{1}{3+1} = \frac{1}{3} - \frac{1}{4}$$

$$\frac{1}{n} = \frac{1}{2n} + \frac{1}{2n} \qquad \Rightarrow \qquad \frac{1}{3} = \frac{1}{2\times3} + \frac{1}{2\times3} = \frac{1}{6} + \frac{1}{6}$$

$$\frac{1}{n(n+k)} = \frac{1}{k}(\frac{1}{n} - \frac{1}{n+k}) \qquad \Rightarrow \qquad \frac{1}{3(3+2)} = \frac{1}{2}(\frac{1}{3} - \frac{1}{5})$$

Example 4. Find the sum: $\dfrac{1}{1\times3} + \dfrac{1}{3\times5} + \cdots + \dfrac{1}{11\times13}$.

Solution: $\dfrac{6}{13}$.

$$\frac{1}{1\times3} + \frac{1}{3\times5} + \cdots + \frac{1}{11\times13} = \frac{1}{2}(\frac{1}{1} - \frac{1}{3} + \frac{1}{3} - \frac{1}{5} + \frac{1}{5} - \ldots + \frac{1}{11} - \frac{1}{13}) = \frac{1}{2}\times(1 - \frac{1}{13}) = \frac{6}{13}$$

Example 5. Calculate: $\dfrac{1}{2\times4} + \dfrac{1}{4\times6} + \cdots + \dfrac{1}{98\times100}$.

Solution: $\dfrac{49}{200}$.

$$\frac{1}{2\times4} + \frac{1}{4\times6} + \cdots + \frac{1}{98\times100}$$

$$= \frac{1}{2}(\frac{1}{2} - \frac{1}{4} + \frac{1}{4} - \frac{1}{6} + \frac{1}{6} - \ldots + \frac{1}{98} - \frac{1}{100}) = \frac{1}{2}\times(\frac{1}{2} - \frac{1}{100}) = \frac{1}{2}(\frac{50}{100} - \frac{1}{100}) = \frac{49}{200}$$

3.3. Continued Fractions

The simple continued fraction representation of a number is given by:

$$a_0 + \cfrac{1}{a_1 + \cfrac{1}{a_2 + \cfrac{1}{a_3 + \cfrac{1}{a_4 + \dots}}}}$$

where a_0 is an integer, any other a_i members are positive integers, and n is a non-negative integer.

Example 6. Simplify: $1 + \cfrac{1}{1 + \cfrac{1}{1 + 1}}$. Express your answer as a common fraction.

Solution: $1 + \cfrac{1}{1 + \cfrac{1}{1 + 1}} = 1 + \cfrac{1}{1 + \cfrac{1}{2}} = 1 + \cfrac{1}{\frac{3}{2}} = 1 + \frac{2}{3} = \frac{5}{3}$

Example 7. Simplify: $\cfrac{1}{2 + \cfrac{1}{2 + \cfrac{1}{2}}}$. Express your answer as a common fraction.

Solution: $\cfrac{1}{2 + \cfrac{1}{2 + \cfrac{1}{2}}} = \cfrac{1}{2 + \cfrac{1}{\frac{5}{2}}} = \cfrac{1}{2 + \frac{2}{5}} = \cfrac{1}{\frac{12}{5}} = \frac{5}{12}$

3.4. Fraction Related to Geometry

☆**Example 8.** Six pepperoni circles will exactly fit across the diameter of a 12-inch pizza when placed as shown. If a total of 20 circles of pepperoni are placed on this pizza without overlap, what fraction of the pizza is covered by pepperoni?
(A) 2/3   (B) 5/9   (C) 5/7   (D) 5/6   (E) 23/36.

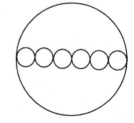

Solution: (B).

If six pepperonis fit across the diameter, then each pepperoni circle has a diameter of 2 inches and a radius of 1 inch. The area of each pepperoni is $\pi\,(1)^2 = \pi$ square inches. The 20 pepperoni circles cover 20π square inches of the pizza. The area of the pizza is $\pi\,(6)^2 = 36\pi$ square inches. The fraction of the pizza covered by pepperoni is $20\pi/36\pi = 5/9$.

Example 9. The area of the figure shown is $\dfrac{11}{5}$. What is the perimeter of the figure?

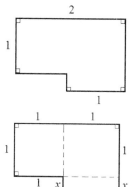

Solution: 32/5 or 6.4

$2 \times 1 + 1 \times x = 11/5$. $x = 1/5$. The perimeter of the figure is $6 + 2x = 6 + 2 \times 1/5 = 6.4$.

Example 10. In the figure shown, all angles are right angles and $y = 2x$. If m, x, and y are lengths of the segments indicated, what fraction of the figure is shaded?

(A) $\dfrac{1}{7}$ (B) $\dfrac{1}{5}$ (C) $\dfrac{1}{14}$ (D) $\dfrac{3}{10}$ (E) $\dfrac{5}{14}$

Solution: (A)

We divided the shape into 28 congruent rectangles. We have 4 shaded. So the fraction is $4/28 = 1/7$.

3.5. Fraction Related to Numbers and Expressions

Example 11. What reduced common fraction is equivalent to $18\dfrac{1}{3}\%$?

Solution: $\dfrac{11}{60}$.

$18\dfrac{1}{3}\% = \dfrac{55}{300} = \dfrac{11}{60}$.

Example 12. If 1/2 + 1/5 + 1/8 > 1/ x + 1/6 + 1/8, then x could not be which of the following?
(A) 1   (B) 2   (C) 3   (D) 4   (E) 8

Solution: (A).
1/2 + 1/5 + 1/8 > 1/ x + 1/6 + 1/8   ⇒   1/2 + 1/5 – 1/6 > 1/ x
8/15 > 1/ x. x should be greater than 15/8 ≈ 1.9.

Example 13. If a and b are integers such that a + b > 160 and a/b = 0.15, what is the smallest possible value of a?
(A) 140   (B) 21   (C) 24   (D) 3   (E) 15

Solution: B.
$\dfrac{a}{b} = 0.15 = \dfrac{15}{100} = \dfrac{3}{20} = \dfrac{18}{120} = \dfrac{21}{140} = \dfrac{24}{160} = ...$ The smallest possible value of a is 21.

Example 14. Which of the following numbers is between $\dfrac{1}{6}$ and $\dfrac{1}{5}$?
(A) 0.14   (B) 0.15   (C) 0.16   (D) 0.17   (E) 0.26

Solution: (D).
1/5 = 0.2 and 1/6 = 0.1$\overline{6}$ > 0.16. the number is between 0.1$\overline{6}$ and 0.2. So the answer is D.

3.6. Fraction Related to Number Lines

Example 15. On the number line shown, the tick marks are equally spaced. What is the value of $w + p$?

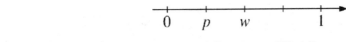

(A) 3/4   (B) 2/3   (C) 1/2   (D) 1/3   (E) 1/4

Solution: (A).

The whole is 4/4. p indicates 1/4 and w indicates 2/4. Therefore $p + w = \dfrac{1}{4} + \dfrac{2}{4} = \dfrac{3}{4}$.

Example 16. Dots are equally spaced on the number line shown. Which of the lettered points has a coordinate equal to $1 - (-\dfrac{1}{2})^2$?

(A) A   (B) B   (C) C   (D) D   (E) E

Solution: D.

$1 - (-\dfrac{1}{2})^2 = 1 - \dfrac{1}{4} = \dfrac{3}{4}$.

The whole part from C to E is 4/4 and D indicates 3/4. So the answer is (D).

3.7. Fraction Applications

Example 17. An hour-long television program included 20 minutes of commercials. What fraction of the hour-long program was not commercials?

Solution: $\dfrac{2}{3}$.

The fraction of the hour-long program was commercials is $\dfrac{20}{60}$. The fraction of the hour-long program was not commercials is $\dfrac{60}{60} - \dfrac{20}{60} = \dfrac{40}{60} = \dfrac{4}{6} = \dfrac{2}{3}$.

Example 18. A container is $\dfrac{3}{5}$ full of water. If 16 gallons of the water were removed from the container, it would be $\dfrac{1}{3}$ full. How many gallons of water does this container hold when it is completely full?

(A) 20   (B) 35   (C) 40   (D) 60   (E) 90.

Solution: (D).

Let x be number of gallons in the container when it is full.

$$\frac{3}{5}x - 16 = \frac{1}{3}x \quad \Rightarrow \quad \frac{3}{5}x - \frac{1}{3}x = 16 \quad \Rightarrow \quad \frac{4}{15}x = 16 \quad \Rightarrow \quad x = 60.$$

Example 19. Roy planted corn on $\frac{2}{7}$ of his land. If he planted 60 acres of corn, how many acres of land does he have?

(A) 90   (B) $112\frac{1}{2}$ (C) 135   (D) 210   (E) $337\frac{1}{2}$

Solution: D.
Let x be number of acres Roy has.

$$\frac{2}{7} \times x = 60 \quad \Rightarrow \quad x = 210.$$

☆**Example 20.** Peter's family ordered a 12-slice pizza for dinner. Peter ate two slices and shared another slice equally with his brother Tom. What fraction of the pizza did Peter eat?

(A) $\frac{1}{8}$ (B) $\frac{1}{7}$ (C) $\frac{5}{24}$ (D) $\frac{1}{6}$ (E) $\frac{1}{24}$

Solution: (C).
The whole slice that Peter ate was 1/12 of the pizza. His half of the second slice was half of 112 , or 1/24 , of the pizza. The fraction of the pizza that Peter ate was

$$\frac{2}{12} + \frac{1}{24} = \frac{4}{24} + \frac{1}{24} = \frac{5}{24}.$$

.

MORE EXAMPLES

Example 21. The fraction halfway between $\frac{1}{5}$ and $\frac{1}{3}$ (on the number line) is

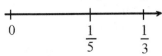

(A) $\dfrac{1}{4}$ (B) $\dfrac{2}{15}$ (C) $\dfrac{4}{15}$ (D) $\dfrac{53}{200}$ (E) $\dfrac{8}{15}$

Solution: C.

$$\dfrac{1}{5}+\dfrac{\frac{1}{3}-\frac{1}{5}}{2}=\dfrac{4}{15}.$$

Example 22. How many more degrees of arc are there in $\dfrac{1}{5}$ of a circle than in $\dfrac{1}{6}$ of circle?

(A) 9°   (B) 12°   (C) 24°   (D) 30°   (E) 36°

Solution: (B).

$$\dfrac{1}{5}\times 360°-\dfrac{1}{6}\times 360°=360°\times(\dfrac{1}{5}-\dfrac{1}{6})=360°\times\dfrac{1}{30}=12°.$$

Example 23. Write the common fraction equivalent to $2\dfrac{1}{2}\%$.

Solution: $\dfrac{1}{40}$

$$2\dfrac{1}{2}\%=\dfrac{5}{2}\times\dfrac{1}{100}=\dfrac{1}{40}.$$

Example 24. If $\dfrac{3}{8}$ of a number is $\dfrac{21}{2}$, what is $\dfrac{1}{7}$ of the number?

(A) 3/2   (B) 9/2   (C) 4   (D) 6   (E) 28

Solution: (C).

Let the number be x. $\dfrac{3}{8}x=\dfrac{21}{2}$ $\Rightarrow$ $x=28$. $\dfrac{1}{7}x=\dfrac{1}{7}\times 28=4$.

Example 25. If 1/4 + 1/5 + 1/6 < 1/5 + 1/6 + 1/y, then y could be which of the following?

(A) 3   (B) 4   (C) 5   (D) 6   (E) 7

Solution: (A).

$1/4 + 1/5 + 1/6 < 1/5 + 1/6 + 1/y \quad \Rightarrow \quad 1/4 < 1/y.$ y should be less than 4.

Example 26. Jenny had a pizza that was divided into 8 equal slices. She ate 3 of them. Alex has a pizza that is the same size, but his is divided into 4 equal slices. He ate 3 slices of his pizza. Who ate more pizza?

Solution: Alex.

$\dfrac{3}{8} < \dfrac{3}{4}$. Alex ate more pizza.

Example 27. Find the sum: $\dfrac{1}{1\times 2} + \dfrac{1}{2\times 3} + \cdots + \dfrac{1}{49\times 50}$.

Solution: $\dfrac{49}{50}$.

$$\dfrac{1}{1\times 2} + \dfrac{1}{2\times 3} + \cdots + \dfrac{1}{49\times 50} = \dfrac{1}{1} - \dfrac{1}{2} + \dfrac{1}{2} - \dfrac{1}{3} + \dfrac{1}{3} - \dfrac{1}{4} + \cdots - \dfrac{1}{50} = 1 - \dfrac{1}{50} = \dfrac{49}{50}$$

Example 28. Simplify: $\dfrac{1}{8 + \dfrac{1}{8 + \dfrac{1}{8}}}$.

Solution:

$$\dfrac{1}{8 + \dfrac{1}{8 + \dfrac{1}{8}}} = \dfrac{1}{8 + \dfrac{1}{\dfrac{65}{8}}} = \dfrac{1}{8 + \dfrac{8}{65}} = \dfrac{1}{\dfrac{528}{65}} = \dfrac{65}{528}.$$

Example 29. If $0 < a < b$, which of the following is greater than b/a?
(A) 1   (B) a/b (C) $1/(b/a)$ (D) $b/2a$ (E) $2b/a$

Solution: E.
Since $0 < a < b$, b/a is a positive number (greater than 1). 2 times a positive number is certainly greater than the number.

PROBLEMS

Problem 1. In the figure below, the measure of $\angle SQR$ is 2/5 the measure of $\angle PQR$. If the measure of $\angle PQR$ is 2/3 the measure of a right angle, what is the measure of $\angle SQP$?

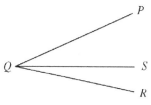

Note: Figure not drawn to scale.

(A) 24°   (B) 36°   (C) 48°   (D) 60°   (E) 96°

Problem 2. If $1/7 + 1/8 + 1/9 > 1/x + 1/8 + 1/9$, then x could be which of the following?
(A) 4   (B) 5   (C) 6   (D) 7   (E) 8

Problem 3. If $1/4 + 1/5 + 1/6 < 1/5 + 1/y + 1/8$, then y could be which of the following?
(A) 3   (B) 4   (C) 5   (D) 6   (E) 7

Problem 4. If a and b are integers such that $a + b < 133$ and $a/b = 0.2$, what is the greatest possible value of b?

Problem 5. If $x = \dfrac{1}{3}$, what is the value of $\dfrac{1}{x} + \dfrac{1}{x-1}$?
(A) −3/2   (B) 3/2   (C) 1   (D) 2   (E) 3

Problem 6. If x, x^2, and x^3 lie on a number line in the order shown below, which of the following could be the value of x?

$$x \qquad x^3 \qquad x^2$$

(A) −2   (B) $-\dfrac{1}{2}$ (C) $\dfrac{2}{3}$ (D) 1   (E) $\dfrac{3}{2}$

Problem 7. If the tick marks on the number line below are equally spaced, which of the lettered points A through E is between 1/4 and 3/8?

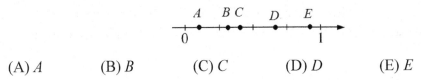

(A) A (B) B (C) C (D) D (E) E

Problem 8. Bob is bakes two pans of brownies that are the same size. One pan has nuts in it and the other pan does not. He cuts the pan with nuts into 8 equal pieces. He cuts the pan without nuts into 16 equal pieces. His friends eat 2 brownies with nuts and 3 brownies without nuts. Did they eat more of the brownies with nuts or without nuts?

Problem 9. On a blueprint, $\dfrac{1}{4}$ inch represents 16 feet, If a driveway is 80 feet long, what is its length, in inches, on the map?

(A) $\dfrac{3}{4}$ (B) $\dfrac{5}{8}$ (C) $\dfrac{5}{4}$ (D) $2\dfrac{1}{2}$ (E) 20

Problem 10. Of all the students in a high school, on a certain day $\dfrac{3}{5}$ rode the bus to school, $\dfrac{3}{10}$ rode in a car, and the remaining students walked. What fraction of the school's students walked to school on that day?

Problem 11. Find the sum $\dfrac{1}{1\times2}+\dfrac{1}{2\times3}+\cdots+\dfrac{1}{100\times101}$.

Problem 12. Calculate: $\dfrac{3}{1\times4}+\dfrac{3}{4\times7}+\dfrac{3}{7\times10}+\cdots+\dfrac{3}{19\times22}$.

Problem 13. Find the sum: $\dfrac{1}{1\times3}+\dfrac{1}{3\times5}+\cdots+\dfrac{1}{1997\times1999}$.

Problem 14. Express as a simplified mixed number: $3 + \dfrac{2}{3 + \dfrac{2}{3 + \dfrac{2}{3}}}$.

Problem 15. In a poll, 45 people were in favor of building a new library, 27 people were against it, and 3 people had no opinion. What fraction of those polled were in favor of building a new library?

(A) $\dfrac{7}{10}$ (B) $\dfrac{3}{5}$ (C) $\dfrac{3}{7}$ (D) $\dfrac{1}{3}$ (E) $\dfrac{3}{10}$

Problem 16. Express as a common fraction: $\dfrac{1}{1 + \dfrac{1}{5}}$.

Problem 17. Express the value of the following expression as a common fraction.

$$1 + \dfrac{2}{3 + \dfrac{4}{5}}$$

Problem 18. Simplify the following and express as a mixed number. $1 + \dfrac{1}{1 + \dfrac{1}{1 + \dfrac{1}{3}}}$.

Problem 19. By 7:00 A.M., 1/5 of the junior class had arrived at a school dance. By 8:00 A.M., 60 more juniors had arrived, raising attendance to 1/3 of the junior class. How many people are in the junior class?

(A) 90   (B) 120   (C) 180   (D) 380   (E) 450

Problem 20. On a hike, Ian walked downhill $\dfrac{3}{7}$ of the time and uphill $\dfrac{4}{7}$ of the time. His downhill walking rate was 5 miles per hour, and his uphill walking rate was 3 miles per hour. The distance that Ian walked downhill was what fraction of the total distance that he walked?

(A) $\dfrac{4}{7}$ (B) $\dfrac{3}{7}$ (C) $\dfrac{2}{5}$ (D) $\dfrac{5}{9}$ (E) $\dfrac{7}{9}$

Problem 21. On each of the days Monday through Thursday, Toni spent 2 hour commuting to work and 1 hour commuting back home. What fraction of the total number of hours in these four days did she spend commuting?

(A) $\dfrac{1}{12}$ (B) $\dfrac{1}{24}$ (C) $\dfrac{5}{12}$ (D) $\dfrac{5}{24}$ (E) $\dfrac{1}{8}$

Problem 22. If the value of $1/t + 5$ is twice the value of $1/t - 1$, what is 7/2 of the value of t ?

Problem 23. If x, x^2, and x^5 lie on a number line in the order shown below, which of the following could be the value of x?

$$x^5 \qquad x^2 \qquad x$$

(A) -2 (B) $-\dfrac{1}{2}$ (C) $\dfrac{2}{3}$ (D) 1   (E) $\dfrac{3}{2}$

Problem 24. On the number line below, the tick marks are equally spaced. What is the value of $x - y$?

$$0 \quad x \qquad y \qquad 1$$

(A) 4/5   (B) 3/4   (C) 2/5   (D) 1/4   (E) 1/5

Problem 25. If a cake is cut into thirds and each third is cut into sevenths, how many pieces of cake are there?

Problem 26. A company sells boxes of balloons in which the balloons are red, green, or blue. Luann purchased a box of balloons in which $\dfrac{1}{5}$ of them were red. If there were half as many green balloons in the box as red ones and 21 balloons were blue, how many balloons were in the box?

SOLUTIONS

Problem 1. Solution: (B).
Since the measure of $\angle SQR$ is 2/5 the measure of $\angle PQR$, the measure of $\angle SQP$ is $(1 - 2/5) = 3/5$ of the measure of $\angle PQR$. So $\angle SQP = 3/5 \times \angle PQR = 3/5 \times 2/3 \times 90° = 36°$.

Problem 12. Solution: (E).

$1/7 + 1/8 + 1/9 > 1/x + 1/8 + 1/9$ $\Rightarrow$ $1/7 > 1/x$. x should be greater than 7.

Problem 3. Solution: (A).
$1/4 + 1/5 + 1/6 < 1/5 + 1/y + 1/8$ $\Rightarrow$ $1/4 + 1/6 - 1/8 < 1/y \Rightarrow$ $7/24 <$ $1/y$ $\Rightarrow$ $y < 24/7$. So y should be less than $24/7 \approx 3.4$.

Problem 4. Solution: $\dfrac{a}{b} = 0.2 = \dfrac{2}{10} = \dfrac{20}{100} = \dfrac{22}{110}$. The greatest possible value of b is 110.

Problem 5. Solution: (B). $\dfrac{1}{x} + \dfrac{1}{x-1} = \dfrac{1}{\dfrac{1}{3}} + \dfrac{1}{\dfrac{1}{3} - 1} = 3 - \dfrac{3}{2} = \dfrac{3}{2}$.

Problem 6. Solution: (B).
Since $x < x^2$, we know that either $x < 0$ or $x > 1$. $x > 1$ is not true since $x^2 < x^3$. So $x < 0$.
Since $x < x^3$, we know that $x > -1$. So the answer is (B).

Problem 7. Solution: (B).
The whole is 4/4. 3/8 is less than 4/8. So $1/4 < B < C < 4/8$. We are not sure if point C is outside 3/8 or not. So the best choice is (B).

Problem 8. Solution: $\dfrac{2}{8} > \dfrac{3}{16}$. They eat more of the brownies.

Problem 9. Solution:

Let x be length on map. $\dfrac{\frac{1}{4}}{16}=\dfrac{x}{80}$ $\qquad\Rightarrow\qquad$ $x=80\times\dfrac{\frac{1}{4}}{16}=\dfrac{20}{16}=\dfrac{5}{4}$.

Problem 10. Solution: 1/10.

Let x be number of students in total, w be number of students walked.

$$\frac{3}{5}x+\frac{3}{10}x+w=x \qquad\Rightarrow\qquad w=x-\frac{3}{5}x-\frac{3}{10}x=(1-\frac{3}{5}-\frac{3}{10})x=\frac{1}{10}x.$$

Problem 11. Solution: 100/101.

$$\frac{1}{1\times2}+\frac{1}{2\times3}+\cdots+\frac{1}{10\times11}=\frac{1}{1}-\frac{1}{2}+\frac{1}{2}-\frac{1}{3}+\frac{1}{3}-\frac{1}{4}+\cdots-\frac{1}{101}=1-\frac{1}{101}=\frac{100}{101}$$

Problem 12. Solution:

$$\frac{3}{1\times4}+\frac{3}{4\times7}+\frac{3}{7\times10}+\cdots+\frac{3}{19\times22}=\frac{1}{1}-\frac{1}{4}+\frac{1}{4}-\frac{1}{7}+\frac{1}{7}\cdots-\frac{1}{19}+\frac{1}{19}-\frac{1}{22}=1-\frac{1}{22}=\frac{21}{22}$$

Problem 13. Solution: 999/1999.

$$\frac{1}{1\times3}+\frac{1}{3\times5}+\cdots+\frac{1}{1997\times1999}=\frac{1}{2}(\frac{1}{1}-\frac{1}{3}+\frac{1}{3}-\frac{1}{5}+\frac{1}{5}-\cdots+\frac{1}{1997}-\frac{1}{1999})=\frac{1}{2}\times\frac{1998}{1999}=\frac{999}{1999}$$

Problem 14. Solution:

$$3+\cfrac{2}{3+\cfrac{2}{3+\cfrac{2}{3}}}=3+\cfrac{2}{3+\cfrac{2}{\frac{11}{3}}}=3+\cfrac{2}{3+\cfrac{6}{11}}=3+\cfrac{2}{\frac{39}{11}}=3\frac{22}{39}.$$

Problem 15. Solution: (B). $\dfrac{45}{45+27+3}=\dfrac{45}{75}=\dfrac{9}{15}=\dfrac{3}{5}$.

Problem 16. Solution: $\dfrac{1}{1+\frac{1}{5}}=\dfrac{1}{\frac{6}{5}}=\dfrac{5}{6}$

Problem 17. Solution: $1 + \dfrac{2}{3 + \dfrac{4}{5}} = 1 + \dfrac{2}{\dfrac{19}{5}} = 1 + \dfrac{10}{19} = \dfrac{29}{19}$

Problem 18. Solution: $1 + \dfrac{1}{1 + \dfrac{1}{1 + \dfrac{1}{3}}} = 1 + \dfrac{1}{1 + \dfrac{1}{\dfrac{4}{3}}} = 1 + \dfrac{1}{1 + \dfrac{3}{4}} = 1 + \dfrac{1}{\dfrac{7}{4}} = 1 + \dfrac{4}{7} = 1\dfrac{4}{7}$.

Problem 19. Solution: (E).
Let x be number of students in the junior class.

$$\frac{1}{5}x + 60 = \frac{1}{3}x \quad \Rightarrow \quad \frac{1}{3}x - \frac{1}{5}x = 60 \quad \Rightarrow \quad \frac{2}{15}x = 60 \quad \Rightarrow \quad x = 450.$$

Problem 20. Solution: (D).
Let t be number of hours Ian walked.

Time used for walking downhill: $\dfrac{3}{7}t$, distance walked downhill: $\dfrac{3}{7}t \times 5$.

Time used for walking uphill: $\dfrac{4}{7}t$, distance walked uphill: $\dfrac{4}{7}t \times 3$.

The ratio of the distance that Ian walked downhill to the total distance that he walked:

$$\frac{\dfrac{3}{7}t \times 5}{\dfrac{3}{7}t \times 5 + \dfrac{4}{7}t \times 3} = \frac{15}{15 + 12} = \frac{15}{27} = \frac{5}{9}.$$

Problem 21. Solution: (E).
The fraction of the total number of hours in one day she spends commuting is $2/24 = 1/8$ which does not change no matter in how many days.

Problem 22. Solution:
$1/t + 5 = 2(1/t - 1) \quad \Rightarrow \quad t = 1/7. \quad \Rightarrow \quad (7/2) \times t = 1/2$.

Problem 23. Solution: C.
Since $x^2 < x$, x, is smaller than 1 but positive. So the answer is (C).

Problem 24. Solution: (C).

The whole is 5/5. x indicates 1/5 and y indicates 3/5. Therefore $y - x = \dfrac{3}{5} - \dfrac{1}{5} = \dfrac{2}{5}$.

Problem 25. Solution: 21.

$\dfrac{1}{3} \times \dfrac{1}{7} = \dfrac{1}{21}$. Therefore we get a total of 21 pieces.

Problem 26. Solution: 30.

Let x be number of balloons in the box.

Red: $\dfrac{1}{5}x$; Green: $\dfrac{1}{2} \times \dfrac{1}{5}x$; and Blue: 21.

So we have $\dfrac{1}{5}x + \dfrac{1}{2} \times \dfrac{1}{5}x + 21 = x \qquad \Rightarrow \qquad x = 30.$

1. BASIC KNOWLEDGE

Even integer:

An integer with the last digit of 0, 2, 4, 6, or 8. General form: $2n$ or $2n + 2$, where n is any integer.

Examples: Even integers: 10, 12, 14, 16, and 18.

Odd integers:

An integer with the last digit of 1, 3, 5, 7, or 9. General form: $2n + 1$ or $2n - 1$.

Examples: Odd integers: 11, 13, 15, 17, and 19.

Parity:

An even number has even parity and an odd number has odd parity.

Properties:

even + even = even.	$12 + 14 = 26$.
even + odd = odd.	$12 + 13 = 25$
odd + odd = even.	$13 + 13 = 26$
odd × odd = odd.	$15 \times 15 = 225$
odd ÷ odd = odd.	$1001 \div 11 = 91$
odd × even = even.	$11 \times 12 = 132$
odd ≠ even.	$1 \neq 2$

2. PROBLEM SOLVING SKILLS

The sum of any even integer and 1 is odd: $4 + 1 = 5$.

The sum of two consecutive integers is odd: $n + (n + 1) = 2n + 1$; $12 + 13 = 25$.

The product of two consecutive integers is even: $n(n + 1)$; $12 \times 13 = 156$.

Any two consecutive integers have opposite parity: 12 is even and 13 odd.
$a + b$ and $a - b$ have the same parity: $15 - 5 = 10$ even; $15 + 5 = 20$ even.

If the product of n positive integers is even, at least one of these n positive integers is even.

If the product of n positive integers is odd, all of these n positive integers are odd.

If the number of odd integers is even, then the sum of them is even.

If the number of odd integers is odd, then the sum of them is odd.

Example 1. Add any 30 consecutive positive integers together. Is the sum even or odd?

Solution: Odd.
There are 15 even and 15 odd positive integers among these 30 positive integers. The sum of 15 even positive integers is even. The sum of 15 odd integers is odd. The final answer is: even + odd = odd.

Example 2. 300 is the sum of 15 consecutive even positive integers. What is the greatest even positive integer among them?

Solution: 34.
The middle number in these 15 integers is the average of them, which is $300/15 = 20$. Because the integers increase by 2, the greatest even number will be $7 \times 2 = 14$ more than the middle number. The answer is $20 + 14 = 34$.

Example 3. The sequence 1, 1, 2, 3, 5, 8, 13, 21, … is formed like this: any term is the sum of the two terms before it, starting from the third term. How many are even numbers of the first 63 terms of the sequence?

Solution: 21.

The numbers are listed as: odd, odd, even; odd, odd, even;... There is one even number in every three consecutive terms. $63/3 = 21$, so there are 21 sets of three terms. Since each set has one even number, there are 21 even numbers.

Example 4. All the positive even integers greater than 0 are arranged in five columns (*A, B, C, D,* and *E*) as shown. Continuing the pattern, in what column will the integer 50 be?

Solution: *B.*

Method 1: Every row has 4 even integers. 50 is the $50/2 = 25^{th}$ even integer. $25 = 4 \times 6 + 1$. So 50 is the first term in the 7th row. The first term in an odd numbered row is in the column B, so 50 is in column *B.*

A	B	C	D	E
	2	4	6	8
16	14	12	10	
	18	20	22	24
32	30	28	26	

....

Method 2: We see a pattern for every 8 integers in the table. 50 is the 25th integer and $25 = 3 \times 8 + 1$. This means that 50 is in the same column as the first number in the first row. The answer is *B.*

Example 5. The sum of all multiples of 3 from 20 to 100 is *S.* Is *S* even or odd?

Solution: Even.
Method 1: All the multiples of 3 can be written out as 21, 24, 27, 30, ..., 93, 96, and 99. The odd numbers are 21, 27, 33, 39, 45, ..., 93, and 99, and the number of odd terms is $(99 - 21) \div 6 + 1 = 14$. The sum of these 14 odd integers is even.

Method 2: There are $\left\lfloor \dfrac{100}{3} \right\rfloor = 33$ multiples of 3 from 1 to 100. 16 of them are even and 17 of them are odd. There are $\left\lfloor \dfrac{20}{3} \right\rfloor = 6$ multiples of 3 from 1 to 20. Three of them (3, 9, and 15) are odd. So there are $17 - 3 = 14$ odd numbers that are multiples of 3 and the sum of them is even.

Example 6. Five lamps are arranged in a row as shown in the figure below. Each lamp has its own switch. All five lamps A, B, C, D, and E are now off. Ben starts to turn each switch from A to E and he repeats the pattern (always from A to E in order) until he turns the switches 2012 times. Which lamps are on finally?

A   B   C   D   E

Solution:

If a lamp is switched an even number of times, it does not change its on or off state.

If a lamp is switched an odd number of times, it changes from on to off or from off to on depending on the original on-off position.

$2012 = 5 \times 402 + 2$.
All lamps are switched 402 times except A and B, which is switched 403 times.

A and B are on. Others are off.

Example 7. If x and y are integers and $x^2y^2 + x^3$ is odd, which of the following statements must be true?
I. x^2 is odd.
II. y is odd.
III. $x + y^2$ is odd.
(A) I only   (B) III only   (C) I and II   (D) I and III   (E) II and III

Solution: D.
Since $x^2y^2 + x^3 = x^2(y^2 + x)$ is odd, both factors must be odd, that is both x^2 and $(y^2 + x)$ must be odd. Therefore the answer is (D).

MORE EXAMPLES

Example 8. If a and b are positive integers and $a^2 - b^2 = 7$, what is the value of b?
(A) 3   (B) 4   (C) 5   (D) 6   (E) 7

Solution: A.
We know that $a^2 - b^2 = (a - b)(a + b) = 7$. Since a and b are positive integers, so we have $a - b = 1$ and $a + b = 7$. Subtracting (1) from (2) we get $2b = 3$. So $b = 3$.

Example 9. The lengths of the sides of a right triangle are consecutive even integers, and the hypotenuse of the right triangle is x. Which of the following equations could be used to find x?
(A) $x + x - 1 = x - 2$ (B) $x^2 + (x - 1)^2 = (x - 2)^2$
(C) $x^2 = (x - 2)^2 + (x - 4)^2$ (D) $x + x + 2 = x + 4$
(E) $x^2 = (x - 2)(x - 4)$

Solution: (C).
The hypotenuse of the right triangle is x. The two legs are $(x - 2)$ and $(x - 4)$, respectively. By the Pythagorean Theorem, we have $x^2 = (x - 2)^2 + (x - 4)^2$. So (C) is the answer.

Example 10. If a and b are positive consecutive odd integers, which of the following must be a positive odd integer?

(A) $a + b$ (B) $a - b$ (C) $2a + b$ (D) $2a - 2b$ (E) $\dfrac{a+b}{2}$

Solution: (C).
We know that odd + odd = even. Since $2a$ is even and b is odd, $2a + b$ must be odd.
We see that others are not necessarily true if we plug in $a = 3$ and $b = 1$ into them.

Example 11. If x and y are positive consecutive odd integers, where $y > x$, which of the following is equal to $y^2 - x^2$?
(A) $6y$ (B) $8y$ (C) $4(y - 2)$ (D) $2y - 1$ (E) $4(y - 1)$

Solution: (E).

Method 1: We see that E is correct and others are not necessarily true if we plug in $y = 3$ and $x = 1$ into them.

Method 2:

Let $y^2 = (2n + 1)^2$ and $x^2 = (2n - 1)^2$.

$y^2 - x^2 = (2n + 1)^2 - (2n - 1)^2 = 4n^2 + 4n + 1 - (4n^2 - 4n + 1) = 8n = 8(y - 1)/2$
$= 4(y - 1)$.

Example 12. The sequence 1, 1, 2, 4, 7, 13, 24, … is formed like this: any term is the sum of the three terms before it starting from the fourth term. Is the 100th term even or odd in the sequence?

Solution: Even.

We see that the pattern is OOEE. $100 = 4 \times 25$. So 100th term has the same property as the fourth term, that is even.

O	O	E	E	(odd + odd + even = even)
1	1	2	4	

	O	E	E	O	(odd + even + even = odd)
	1	2	4	7	

		E	E	O	O	(even + even + odd = odd)
		2	4	7	13	

O	O	E	E	O	O	E	E	
1	1	2	4	7	13	24	44	…

Example 13. The sequence 1, 1, 2, 3, 5, 8, 13, 21, … is formed like this: any term is the sum of the two terms before it, starting from the third term. How many odd numbers are there in the first 900 terms of the sequence?

Solution: 600.

The numbers are listed in the following pattern: odd, odd, even; odd, odd, even;...
There are two odd numbers in every consecutive three terms. $900/3 = 300$. There are 300 sets of three terms and each set has two odd numbers. There are $300 \times 2 = 600$ odd numbers.

Example 14. Mr. Mathis and his student Peter worked together to solve math problems last week. When each person solved a problem, that person put a marble in his own box. Mr. Mathis's problem solving speed was half of his student. At the end of the problem solving session, Peter had four boxes of marbles and Mr. Mathis had two boxes of marbles. Each box is labeled with the number of marbles inside it. The numbers are 78, 94, 86, 87, 82, and 80, respectively. Which two boxes belong to Mr. Mathis?

Solution: boxes labeled 87 and 82.

The sum of marbles is $78 + 94 + 86 + 82 + 80 = 507$. Since Peter's speed is twice of Mr. Mathis's speed, the number of Mr. Mathis's marbles is $507/3 = 169$, which is an odd number. The box labeled 87 is one of Mr. Mathis's boxes. The other box should be $169 - 87 = 82$. So boxes labeled 87 and 82 belong to Mr. Mathis.

Example 15. All the positive integers greater than 1 are arranged in five columns (A, B, C, D, E) as shown. Continuing the pattern, in what column will the integer 800 be written?

	A	B	C	D	E
Row 1		2	3	4	5
Row 2	9	8	7	6	
Row 3		10	11	12	13
Row 4	17	16	15	14	
Row 5		18	19	20	21

(A) *A*   (B) *B*   (C) *C*   (D) *D*   (E) *E*

Solution:

Method 1: Every row has 2 even integers. 800 is the $800/2 = 400^{th}$ even integer. $400 = 2 \times 200$, so 800 is the last even term in 200th row, and also in the same column as the last even number in the 2nd row. 800 is in column B.

Method 2: We see the pattern for every 8 integers (every four even integers) in the table. 800 is the 800th integers and $800 = 8 \times 100$. So 800 is in the same column as the last even number in the second row. The answer is B.

Example 16. Five lamps are arranged in a row as shown in the figure below. Each lamp has its own switch. All five lamps A, B, C, D, and E are now off. Ben starts to turn each switch from A to E and he repeats the pattern (always from A to E in order) until he turns the switches 126 times. Which lamps are on in the end?

| A | B | C | D | E |

Solution: B, C, D and E.
If a lamp is switched an even number of times, it does not change its on or off state.
If a lamp is switched an odd number of times, it changes from on to off or from off to on depending on the original on-off position.

$126 = 5 \times 25 + 1$.

All lamps are switched 25 times except A, which is switched 26 times.

So lamp A is still off and all others are on.

PROBLEMS

Problem 1. If a and b are positive integers and $a^2 - b^2 = 143$, what is the value of a?

(A) 1   (B) 11   (C) 12   (D) 13   (E) 14

Problem 2. The lengths of the sides of a right triangle are consecutive even integers, and the length of the longer leg is x. Which of the following equations could be used to find x?

(A) $x + x + 1 = x + 2$ (B) $x^2 + (x + 1)^2 = (x + 2)^2$
(C) $(x - 2)^2 + x^2 = (x + 2)^2$ (D) $x - 2 + x = x + 2$
(E) $x^2 = (x - 2)(x + 2)$

Problem 3. If a and b are positive odd integers, which of the following must be a positive even integer?

(A) $a + b$ (B) $a - b$ (C) $2a + b$ (D) $2a - b$ (E) $\dfrac{a + b}{2}$

Problem 4. If x and y are positive consecutive even integers, where $y > x$, which of the following is equal to $y^2 - x^2$?

(A) $2x$ (B) $4x$ (C) $2x + 2$ (D) $2x + 4$ (E) $4x + 4$

Problem 5. If x and y are positive consecutive odd integers, where $y > x$, which of the following is equal to $y^2 - x^2 + 8$?

(A) $6x$ (B) $8x$ (C) $2x + 2$ (D) $2x + 4$ (E) $4(x + 3)$

Problem 6. If a and b are odd integers, which of the following must also be an odd integer?

I. $(a + 2)b$ II. $(a + 2) + b$ III. $(a + 2) - b$

(A) I only   (B) II only   (C) III only   (D) I and II   (E) II and III

Problem 7. If t represents an odd integer, which of the following expressions represents an even integer?

(A) $t + 4$ (B) $2t - 3$ (C) $3t - 6$ (D) $3t + 8$ (E) $5t + 5$

Problem 8. If $\dfrac{x+7}{2}$ is an integer. Then x must be

(A) a negative integer   (B) a positive integer   (C) a multiple of 3
(D) an even integer   (E) an odd integer

Problem 9. If k is a positive integer, which of the following must represent an odd integer that is twice the value of an odd integer?
(A) $4k + 3$ (B) $2k + 3$ (C) $2k + 4$ (D) $4k + 1$ (E) $4k + 2$

Problem 10. If k is a negative even integer and n is a positive odd integer, which of the following could be equal to $n - k$?
I. 0   II. 1   III. 3.

(A) I only   (B) II only   (C) III only   (D) I and III only   (E) I, II, and III

Problem 11. The sum of the positive odd integers less than 1000 is subtracted from the sum of the positive even integers less than or equal to 1000. What is the resulting difference?

Problem 12. Each of the 75 children in a line was assigned one of the integers from 1 through 99 by counting off in order. Then, standing in the same order, the children counted off in the opposite direction, so that the child who was assigned the number 99 the first time was assigned the number 1 the second time. Which of the following is a pair of numbers assigned to the same child?
(A) 50 and 48   (B) 49 and 50   (C) 66 and 33   (D) 33 and 67   (E) 45 and 32

Problem 13. The counting numbers are arrange in four columns as shown below. Under which column letter will 2012 appear?

```
A  B  C  D
1  2  3  4
8  7  6  5
9  10 11 12
   ... 14 13
```

Problem 14. Suppose all the counting numbers are arranged in columns as shown below. Under what column-letter will 2012 appear?

```
A   B   C   D   E   F   G
1   2   3   4   5   6   7
8   9   10  11  12  13  14
15  16  17  18  19  _   _
```

Problem 15. Is $1 + 2 + 3 + 4 + ... + 2011 + 2012$ even or odd?

Problem 16. Is the expression $1 \times 2 + 3 \times 4 + 5 \times 6 + ... + 99 \times 100$ even or odd?

Problem 17. Seven lamps labeled A through G are arranged in a row. Each lamp has its own switch. Now lamps A, C, E, and G are on and other lamps are off. Ben starts to flip each switch from A to G the following way: if the lamp is on, he turns it off; if the lamp is off, he turns it on. He repeats the pattern until he flips the switches 2011 times. Which lamps are on finally?

SOLUTIONS

Problem 1. Solution: C.
We know that $a^2 - b^2 = (a - b)(a + b) = 143 = 11 \times 13$. Since a and b are positive integers, so we have $a - b = 11$ and $a + b = 13$. Adding them we get $2a = 24$. So $a = 12$.

Problem 2. Solution: (C).
The longer leg is x. The shorter leg is $(x - 2)$ and the hypotenuse of the right triangle is $(x + 2)$, respectively. By the Pythagorean Theorem, we have $x^2 + (x - 2)^2 = (x + 4)^2$. So (C) is the answer.

Problem 3. Solution: (A).
We know that odd + odd = even. So we know that (A) must be the correct answer. We see that others are not necessarily true if we plug in $a = 1$ and $b = 1$ into them.

Problem 4. Solution: E.
Method 1: We see that E is correct and others are not necessarily true if we plug in $y = 4$ and $x = 2$ into them.

Method 2: Let $y^2 = (2n)^2$ and $x^2 = (2n - 2)^2$.
$y^2 - x^2 = (2n)^2 - (2n - 2)^2 = 4n^2 - (4n^2 - 8n + 4) = 8n - 4 = 8(x + 2)/2 - 4 = 4(x + 2) - 4 = 4x + 4$.

Problem 5. Solution: (E).
Method 1: We see that E is correct and others are not necessarily true if we plug in $y = 3$ and $x = 1$ into them.

Method 2:
Let $y^2 = (2n + 1)^2$ and $x^2 = (2n - 1)^2$.
$y^2 - x^2 + 8 = (2n + 1)^2 - (2n - 1)^2 + 8 = 4n^2 + 4n + 1 - (4n^2 - 4n + 1) + 8 = 8n + 8 = 8(x+1)/2 + 8 = 4(x+1) + 8 = 4(x+3)$.

Problem 6. Solution: E.
I. $(a + 2)b = ab + 2b = $ odd + even = odd.
II. $(a + 2) + b = (a + b) + 2 = $ odd + odd + even = even + even = even

III.$(a + 2) - b = (a - b) + 2$ = odd – odd + even = even + even = even
The answer is then (A).

Problem 7. Solution: (E).
(A) $t + 4$ = odd + even = odd.   (B) $2t - 3$ = even – odd = odd.
(C) $3t - 6$ = odd – even = odd.   (D) $3t + 8$ = odd + even = odd.
(E) $5t + 5$ = odd + odd = even.
The answer is then (E).

Problem 8. Solution: E

Let $\dfrac{x+7}{2} = n \implies x = 2n - 7$ = even – odd = odd.

Problem 9. Solution: A.
The odd integer is $2(2k + 1) + 1 = 4k + 3$.

Problem 10. Solution: C.
Let $k = -2m$. m is an integer. Then $n - k = n - (-2m) = n + 2m$ = odd + even = odd > 1. The answer is C.

Problem 11. Solution:
The sum of positive even integers is $N_1 = 2 + 4 + 6 + \ldots + 1000$ (1)
The sum of positive odd integers is $N_2 = 1 + 3 + 5 + \ldots + 999$ (2)
There are $1000/2 = 500$ terms in each sum.
(1) – (2): $N_1 - N_2 = 1 + 1 + \ldots + 1 = 500$.

Problem 12. Solution: (D). From the list below we see that the sum of two numbers must be 100.

1	2	3	4	5	…	97	98	99
99	98	97	96	95	…	3	2	1

Problem 13. Solution:
Method 1: We know that there are 2 even integers in every row. 2012 is the 1006th even integer. $1006 = 2 \times 503 = 2 \times 502 + 2$. This means that 2012 will be in the column where the 2nd even integer located (even integer 4 in column D, in this case).

Method 2: We see the pattern in every 8 numbers. $2012 = 8 \times 251 + 4$. So 2012 is in the column where the 4th number located (even integer 4 in column D, in this case).

Problem 14. Solution: C.
Method 1: We know that there are 7 even integers every two row. 2012 is the 1006th even integer. $1006 = 7 \times 143 + 5$. This means that 2012 will be in the column where the fifth even integer (10, in this case) located.

Method 2: We see the pattern in every 7 numbers. $2012 = 7 \times 287 + 3$. So 2012 is in the column where the third number located (column C in this case).

Problem 15. Solution: Even.
There are $2012/2 = 1006$ even integers and 1006 odd integers. The sum of 1006 even integers is even. The sum of 1016 odd integers is also even. So the answer is: even.

Problem 16. Solution: even.
Since every product has an even number in it, the expression is even.

Problem 17. Solution: A, D, and F.
If a lamp is switched an even number of times, it does not change the lamp's on or off state.
If a lamp is switched an odd number of times, it changes from on to off or from off to on depending on the original on-off position.
$2011 = 7 \times 287 + 2$
All lamps are switched 287 times except the lamps A and B that are switched 288 times.

	A	B	C	D	E	F	G
Start	on	Off	on	Off	on	off	On
End	on	Off	off	on	off	on	off

1. BASIC KNOWLEDGE

Terms

A percent is a ratio that compares a number to 100. It also means hundredths, or per hundred. The symbol for percent is %.

Note: The word "percent" consists of two parts: per and cent. Per means "divide by" and *cent* means "hundred."

Percent is a special form of decimals and a more special form of fractions. For example, $50\% = \dfrac{50}{100} = 0.5$.

All the operation rules of decimals and fractions will apply to percent.

Percent of change: A number is changed from the value of *a* to the value of *b*,

if $b > a$, the percent of change (increase) is $\dfrac{b-a}{a} \times 100\%$.

if $b < a$, the percent of change (decrease) is $\dfrac{a-b}{a} \times 100\%$.

Basic types of percent problems

$\dfrac{x}{b} = \dfrac{c}{100}$ $\Rightarrow$ $x = \dfrac{c}{100}b$		What number is c % of b?
$\dfrac{a}{b} = \dfrac{x}{100}$ $\Rightarrow$ $a = \dfrac{x}{100}b$		a is what % of b?
$\dfrac{a}{x} = \dfrac{c}{100}$ $\Rightarrow$ $a = \dfrac{c}{100}x$		a is c % of what number?

Translation of words to math symbols

Word form	Math symbol	Meaning
what number	x	unknown symbol
is	$=$	equals
of	$\times$	multiplication

2. PROBLEM SOLVING SKILLS

2.1. Percent of A Number

Example 1. Of the 24 members of a class, 25% are seniors. How many members are not seniors?

Solution: 18.

$$24 - \frac{25}{100} \times 24 = 24 - 6 = 18.$$

Example 2. What number is 25% of 3500?

Solution: 875.

Let x be the number: $x = \frac{25}{100} \times 3500 = 875$.

Example 3. Erica has saved $63 toward the purchase of a $300 camera. What percent of the total price has she saved?

Solution: 21%.

This question is the same as to ask: 63 is what percent of 300?

Method 1: $\frac{63}{300} = \frac{3 \times 21}{3 \times 100} = \frac{21}{100} = 21\%$.

Method 2: 63 is x percent of 300: $63 = \dfrac{x}{100} \times 300$ $\Rightarrow$ $x = \dfrac{63}{3} = 21$ percent.

Example 4. 25% of what number is 30?

Solution: 120.

$\dfrac{25}{100} \times x = 30$ $\Rightarrow$ $x = 120$.

Example 5. 3 is 0.4% of what number?

Solution: 750.

$3 = \dfrac{0.4}{100} \times x$ $\Rightarrow$ $x = 750$.

Example 6. 12 is what percent of 20?

Solution: 60.

$12 = x\% \times 20$ $\Rightarrow$ $x = 60$.

Example 7. What number is 25% of 1696?

Solution: 424.

$x = 25\% \times 1696$ $\Rightarrow$ $x = \dfrac{1}{4} \times 1696 = 424$.

2.2. Percent Increase and Decrease

Example 8. A student has an average of 85% on 3 one-hour exams. If each counts the same and the final counts twice as much as a one-hour exam, what percent must the student make on the final to have an overall average of 90% for the course?

Solution: 97.5%.

Method 1: If the overall average is 90, the total points will be $5 \times 90 = 450$ (three 85's and two for the final since the final counts twice). $450 - 85 \times 3 = 195$. The final score is $195 / 2 = 97.5$ or 97.5%.

Method 2: Let x be the final percent.

$$\frac{0.85 \times 3 + 2x}{5} = 0.9 \qquad \Rightarrow \qquad x = 0.975 = 97.5\%$$

Example 9. A softball team won seven of its first dozen games. How many of the remaining 20 games does the team have to win to have a season record of winning 75% of its games?

Solution: 17 games.
Method 1: The total games for the season is $12 + 20 = 32$. The total number of games the team won is $\frac{75}{100} \times 32 = 24$. So there are $24 - 7 = 17$ games the team needs to win.

Method 2: Let x be the number of games the team has to win of the remaining 20 games.

$$\frac{7 + x}{12 + 20} = \frac{75}{100} \qquad \Rightarrow \qquad x = 17.$$

2.3 Discounts

Example 10. A worker was taken off the job for the first 40 working days of the year with no pay. If the worker's pay for 200 working days is $22,000, what percent raise must the worker get in order to receive $22,000 over the next 160 working days?

Solution: 25 %.

The number of dollars he earned each day over 160 days is $\frac{22000}{160} = 137.5$.

The number of dollars he earned each day over 200 days is $\frac{22000}{200} = 110$.

The percent raise the worker must get in order to receive $22,000 over the next 160 working is $\dfrac{137.5 - 110}{110} = 0.25 = 25\%$.

Example 11. After a recent diet, a dieter weighed in at 135 lbs. This represented a weight loss of 10% on the pre-diet weight of the dieter. How many pounds did the dieter weigh prior to the diet?

Solution: 150 lbs.

The number of pounds the dieter weighted before is $\dfrac{135}{0.9} = 150$.

2.4 . Discounts on Discounts

Example 12. Given that 1% of 1% of a number is 5, what is the number?

Solution: 50000.

Let the number be x.
$1\% \times 1\% \times x = 5$ $\Rightarrow$ $x = 50000$.

Example 13. In a certain school $37\dfrac{1}{2}\%$ of the students were on the honor roll. Of the students on the honor roll $8\dfrac{1}{3}\%$ had a straight A average. If 58 students had a straight A average, how many students were enrolled in the school?

Solution: 1856 (students).

Let x be the number of students enrolled in the school.
$37\dfrac{1}{2}\% \times x \times 8\dfrac{1}{3}\% = 58$ $\Rightarrow$ $x = 1856$.

Example 14. On Monday, Euler's Bakery discounted the price of pies 20%. On Tuesday, it discounted the pies an additional 70%. What is the combined percent discount?

Solution: 76.

Method 1: The equivalent one single discount is $1 - 0.8 \times 0.3 = 1 - 0.24 = 0.76 = 76\%$.

Method 2: $d = d_1 + d_2 - d_1 \times d_2 = \dfrac{20}{100} + \dfrac{70}{100} - \dfrac{20}{100} \times \dfrac{70}{100} = \dfrac{76}{100}$

Example 15. In 2010 the population of a city was 150,000. If the population increases 5% each year in 2011 and 2012, decreases 4% in 2013, and increases 10% in 2014, what will the population be at the end of 2014?

Solution: 174,636.

$150,000 \times 1.05 \times 1.05 \times 0.96 \times 1.1 = 174636$.

☆**Example 16.** A store advertises that everything is "half price." In addition, a coupon gives a 30% discount on sale prices. With the coupon, the price represents what percentage discount off the original price?
(A) 60   (B) 70   (C) 63   (D) 65   (E) 80

Solution: (D).
The price of an item costing d after both discounts are applied is $0.7(0.5d) = 0.35d$, a discount of 65% off the original price.

2.5. Diluting Solutions

Example 17. Thirty ounces of vinegar with a strength of 30% was mixed with 50 ounces of a 20% vinegar solution. What was the percentage of the resulting solution?

Solution: 23.75%.

We introduce the "C-V-S" method. C is the concentration or the strength of the solution. V is the volume of the solution. S is the substance of the solution.

Note: $C \times V = S$, $V_A + V_B = V_D$, and $S_A + S_B = S_D$. There is no relationship for C_A, C_B, and C_D.

Name	C	$\times$	V	$=$	S
A	0.3	$\times$	30	$=$	$0.3 \times 30 = 9$
			$+$		$+$
B	0.2	$\times$	50	$=$	$0.2 \times 50 = 10$
			$\parallel$		$\parallel$
Mixture	x	$\times$	80	$=$	$80\,x$

$$9 + 10 = 80x \qquad\qquad \Rightarrow x = 0.2375 = 23.75\%.$$

Example 18. How many liters of a 20% alcohol solution must be added to 90 liters of a 50% alcohol solution to form a 45% solution?

Solution: 18 liters.

Name	C	V	S
A	0.2	x	$0.2 \times x$
B	0.5	90	45
Mixture	0.45	$90 + x$	$0.45(90 + x)$

$$0.45(90 + x) = 0.2\,x + 45 \qquad \Rightarrow \qquad x = 18 \text{ liters.}$$

Example 19. How many ounces of pure acid (100%) should be added to 120 fluid ounces of a 20% acid solution to obtain a 40% acid solution?

Solution: 40 liters.

Name	C	V	S
A	1	x	x
B	0.2	120	24
Mixture	0.4	$120 + x$	$0.4(120 + x)$

$$x + 24 = 0.4(120 + x) \Rightarrow \qquad x = 40 \text{ liters.}$$

Example 20. A chemist needs a 15% alcohol solution and has only a 60% solution. How much water should be added to obtain 10 liters of the weaker solution?

Solution: 7.5 liters.

Name	C	V	S
A	0	x	0
B	0.6	y	0.6y
Mixture	0.15	10	1.5

$0.6y = 1.5$ $\Rightarrow$ $y = 2.5.$

$x + y = 10.$ $\Rightarrow$ $x = 7.5.$

Example 21. 100 kg of a fruit contained 90% water one week ago. How many kg of the fruit containing 80% water are there now?

Solution: 50.

Name	C	V	S
A	0.1	100	10
B	0.2	x	0.2 x

The substance does not change before or after the evaporating: $10 = 0.2x$ $\Rightarrow x$ = 50.

3. MORE EXAMPLES

Example 22. If 8.5 is x percent of 85, what is x percent of 20?
(A) 20   (B) 2   (C) 0.75   (D) 0.15   (E) 0.85

Solution: (B).

8.5 is x percent of 85 $\Rightarrow$ $8.5 = \dfrac{x}{100} \times 85$ $\Rightarrow$ $\dfrac{x}{100} = 0.1$

what is x percent of 20 $\Rightarrow$ $y = \dfrac{x}{100} \times 20 = 0.1 \times 20 = 2$.

Example 23. If $x > 0$ and 20 percent of x is equal to 40 percent of y, then 40 percent of x equals what percent of y?
(A) 15%   (B) 50%   (C) 60%   (D) 80%   (E) It cannot be determined without knowing the exact values of x and y.

Solution: (D).
Since 20 percent of x is equal to 40 percent of y, we have:
$$0.2\,x = 0.4y \tag{1}$$
$(1) \times 2$: $0.4x = 0.8y$.
That is, 40 percent of x equals 80 percent of y.

Example 24. The daytime telephone rate between two cities is 80 cents for the first 5 minutes and n cents for each additional minute. The total charge is reduced 85 percent on calls made after 7:00 P.M. The cost, in dollars, of a 60-minute call made at 7:11 P.M. between these two cities is
(A) $0.15(0.80) + 55n$ (B) $0.15(0.80 + 0.55n)$ (C) $0.15(0.80 + 0.60n)$
(D) $0.85(0.80 + 0.55n)$ (E) $0.85(0.80 + 0.60n)$

Solution: (B).
The call during the first 5 minutes costs $0.8 \times (1 - 0.85) = 0.8 \times 0.15$ dollars. The call during the rest of 55 minutes costs $55 \times n \times (1 - 0.85) = 55 \times n \times 0.15$ cents $= 0.55 \times n \times 0.15$ dollars. The total cost is $0.8 \times 0.15 + 0.55 \times n \times 0.15 = 0.15(0.80 + 0.55n)$ dollars.

Example 25. A test has two parts. The first part is worth 60% and the second part is worth 40%. If a student gets 95% of part one correct, what exact percent must this student achieve on part two to average 90% for the whole test?

Solution: 82.5 %.
The points counted toward to final scores the student got for the first test:
$$\frac{60}{100} \times 95 = 57.$$
Let x be the percent the student must get: $57 + 40x = 90 \quad \Rightarrow \quad x = 0.825 = 82.5\%$.

Example 26. A worker gets a 25% increase in salary. If the new salary is $18,750, what was the old salary in dollars?

Solution: 15,000.

Let x be the old salary. $x \times \dfrac{125}{100} = 18750$ $\Rightarrow$ $x = 15000$.

Example 27. The original price of a book was b dollars. This price was discounted x percent during a sale. Alex used a coupon to buy the book for t percent off the sale price. Which of the following represents the dollars, that Alex saved for the book?

(A) $b(1 - \dfrac{x}{100})(1 - \dfrac{t}{100})$ (B) $b[1 - (1 - \dfrac{x}{100})(1 - \dfrac{t}{100})]$ (C) $b(1 - \dfrac{x+t}{100})$

(D) $b(1 - \dfrac{xt}{100})$ (E) $b(\dfrac{x}{100})(\dfrac{t}{100})$.

Solution: (B).

After the first discount, the sale price is $b(1 - \dfrac{x}{100})$.

This price is off by t percent with a coupon. Then the final price will be

$b(1 - \dfrac{x}{100})(1 - \dfrac{t}{100})$.

Alex saved $b - b(1 - \dfrac{x}{100})(1 - \dfrac{t}{100})$ or $b[1 - (1 - \dfrac{x}{100})(1 - \dfrac{t}{100})]$ dollars.

Example 28. A television's price was discounted 40% and then slashed another 40% during a liquidation sale. By what percent has the original price been reduced?

Solution: 64 %.
Method 1: Let x be the original price.
The sale price after two discounts will be:

$\dfrac{60}{100} \times \dfrac{60}{100} \times x = 0.36x$ $\Rightarrow$ $1 - 36\% = 64\%$.

Method 2: The percent reduced: $\dfrac{40}{100} + \dfrac{40}{100} - \dfrac{40}{100} \times \dfrac{40}{100} = \dfrac{64}{100} = 64\%$.

Example 29. The price of an article is cut 10%. To restore it to its former value, the new price must be increased by:

(A) 10%   (B) 9%   (C) $11\frac{1}{9}$%   (D) 11%   (E) none of these answers

Solution: $11\frac{1}{9}$%.

Let M be the marked price of the article. $M - 0.1M = 0.9M =$ new price. To restore $0.9M$ to M requires the addition of $0.1M$. $0.1M = \frac{1}{9}(0.9M)$, and $\frac{1}{9}$,

expressed as a percent, is $11\frac{1}{9}$%.

Example 30. 130 grams of a 5% salt solution are mixed with a 9% of salt solution to make a 6.4% of salt solution. What was the weight, in grams, of the resulting solution?

(A) 200   (B) 190   (C) 180   (D) 170   (E) 130

Solution: (A). 200.

Name	C	V	S
A	0.05	130	6.5
B	0.09	x	$0.09x$
Mixture	0.064	$130 + x$	$0.064(130 + x)$

$6.5 + 0.09x = 0.064(130 + x)$ ⇒ $x = 70$ grams.
The answer is: $130 + 70 = 200$.

PROBLEMS

Problem 1. A box contains 3,900 solid-colored marbles that are either orange, blue, red, or green. If 19 percent of the marbles are orange, 29 percent of the marbles are red, and 39 percent of the marbles are blue, what percent are green?
(A) 13%   (B) 23%   (C) 33%   (D) 58%   (E) 87%

Problem 2. From 1979 to 1989, the total population in the four regions of ABC city increased by approximately what percent?
(A) 50%   (B) 90%   (C) 95%   (D) 100%   (E) 150%

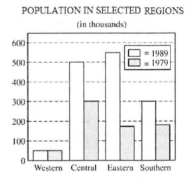

POPULATION IN SELECTED REGIONS
(in thousands)

Problem 3. If 0.05 percent of n is 5, what is 5 percent of n ?
(A) 900   (B) 600   (C) 500   (D) 0.006   (E) 0.003

Problem 4. Sixty percent of the songs played on a certain radio station are 5 minutes long, 30 percent are 8 minutes long, and 10 percent are 6 minutes long. What is the average (arithmetic mean) number of minutes per song played on this radio station?

Problem 5. If the length of a rectangle is increased by 40% and the width of the same rectangle is decreased by 40%, what is the effect on the area of the rectangle?

(A) It is increased by 60%.   (B) It is increased by 30%.   (C) It is unchanged.
(D) It is decreased by 15%.   (E) It is decreased by 9%.

Problem 6. Rita's dog weighed 10 pounds when she bought it. Over the next several years, the dog's weight increased by 11 percent per year. Which of the following functions gives the weight, w, in pounds, of the dog after n years of weight gain at this rate?

(A) $w(n) = 10 + 0.11^n$ (B) $w(n) = 10(0.11)^n$ (C) $w(n) = 10(0.9)^n$

(D) $w(n) = 10(1.11)^n$ (E) $w(n) = 10(n)^{1.11}$

Problem 7. Find $4\frac{1}{2}\%$ of 500. Express your answer as a decimal.

Problem 8. What percent of 500 is 200?

Problem 9. Sixty-four is 25% of what number?

Problem 10. 6000 is $1\frac{1}{2}\%$ of what number?

Problem 11. On an achievement test, ninth graders averaged 93% and eighth graders averaged 75%. A total of 90 students took the test and averaged 87%. How many ninth graders took the test?

Problem 12. A basketball team has played 12 games and won 10 of them. If the team wins $44\frac{4}{9}\%$ of its remaining 18 games, what percent of its games has the team won at the end of the season?

Problem 13. During a sale, all items were marked 40% off. If the sale price of an item was $10.50, what was its original price in dollars?

Problem 14. The price of an article was marked down 35% during a sale. If the sale price was $36.40, what was the price before the sale?

Problem 15. A refrigerator is offered for sale at $250.00 less successive discounts of 20% and 15%. The sale price of the refrigerator is:

(A) 35% less than $250.00   (B) 65% of $250.00   (C) 77% of $250.00
(D) 68% of $250.00   (E) none of these

Problem 16. An item was placed on sale in January for 30% less than its original price. A final close-out sale was offered in February, and the January sale price was reduced by 40%. What percent of the original price was the final reduced price?

Problem 17. An item was placed on sale in January for 30% less than its original price. A final close-out sale was offered in February, and the January sale price was reduced by 40%. What percent of the original price was the final reduced price?

Problem 18. How many dollars would be paid in simple interest if $200 is borrowed at 12% per year for 5 months?

Problem 19. Two high school classes took the same test. One class of 20 students made an average grade of 80%; the other class of 30 students made and average grade of 70% . The average grade for all students in both classes is:
(A) 75%   (B) 74%   (C) 72%   (D) 77%   (E) none of these

Problem 20. A house and store were sold for $12,000 each. The house was sold at a loss of 20% of the cost, and the store at a gain of 20% of the cost. The entire transaction resulted in :
(A) no loss or gain   (B) loss of $1000   (C) gain of $1000
(D) gain of $2000   (E) none of these

Problem 21. A housewife saved $2.50 in buying a dress on sale. If she spent $25 for the dress, she saved about:
(A) 8%   (B) 9%   (C) 10%   (D) 11%   (E) 12%

Problem 22. How much water should be added to 8 liters of 90% alcohol to make a 40% alcohol solution?

Problem 23. How many liters of water should be added to 10 liter of a 20% saline (salt) solution to make a 5% saline solution?

Problem 24. How many grams of 5% salt solution should be added to 500 grams of a 20% salt solution to make a 15% salt solution?

Problem 25. A 30% alcohol solution is added x grams pure water to make a 24% alcohol solution. If x gram pure water is added again to the solution, what was the percentage of the resulting solution?
(A) 30%   (B) 20%   (C) 10%   (D) 8%   (E) 5%

Problem 26. A sort of coals weighed 100 kg contained 14.5% water. After some time evaporating, the water was 10%. What was the ratio of the weight of the coals now to the weight of coals before evaporation?
(A) 19/20   (B) 20/19   (C) 9/10   (D) 8/10   (E) 171/180

Problem 27. A box of staples contains 4,600 staples that are either silver, black, or red. If 46 percent of the staples are silver and 46 percent are black, how many red staples are there?
(A) 2116   (B) 2484   (C) 368   (D) 828   (E) 920

Problem 28. Alex and Betsy are both salespeople. Alex's weekly compensation consists of $800 plus 30 percent of his sales. Betsy's weekly compensation consists of $600 plus 35 percent of her sales. If they both had the same amount of sales and the same compensation for a particular week, what was that compensation, in dollars? (Disregard the dollar sign when recording your answer).

Problem 29. Twenty-four is $8\frac{1}{3}\%$ of what number?

Problem 30. Find $12\frac{1}{2}\%$ of 160.

Problem 31. If q and r are positive numbers, what percent of $(q + r)$ is r ?
(A) $\dfrac{1}{100r(q+r)}\%$ (B) $\dfrac{q+r}{100r}\%$ (C) $\dfrac{100(q+r)}{r}\%$ (D) $(\dfrac{100r}{q}+r)\%$ (E) $\dfrac{100r}{q+r}\%$

Problem 32. On a $10,000 order a merchant has a choice between three successive discounts of 20%, 20%, and 10% and three successive discounts of 40%, 5%, and 5%. By choosing the better offer, he can save:
(A) nothing at all   (B) $400   (C) $330   (D) $345   (E) $360

Problem 33. Ann borrowed $750.00 at a simple interest rate of 7.5% per year. How much will Ann owe after eight months?
(A) 37.50   (B) 795.50   (C) 56.25   (D) 787.50   (E) 800.00

Problem 34. A pharmacist wants to dilute a 10% hydrogen peroxide solution to 3%. How much distilled water must he add to make 10 liters of 3% solution?
(A) 5   (B) 7   (C) 8   (D) 10   (E) 2

SOLUTIONS

Problem 1. Solution:
$100\% - 19\% - 29\% - 39\% = 13\%$.

Problem 2. Solution: (D).
The total population in 1979: $50 + 300 + 170 + 180 = 700$.
The total population in 1989: $50 + 500 + 550 + 300 = 1400$.
The percent of increase is $\dfrac{1400 - 700}{700} = 100\%$.

Problem 3. Solution: (C).

0.05 percent of n is 5 $\qquad \Rightarrow \qquad \dfrac{0.05}{100} \times n = 5 \qquad\qquad (1)$

Multiplying 100 by both sides of (1): $\dfrac{5}{100} \times n = 500$.

What is 5 percent of $n \Rightarrow \qquad y = \dfrac{5}{100} \times n = 500$.

Problem 4. Solution:
Let x be the number of songs. The average number of minutes per song played on this radio station is
$$\frac{0.6x \times 5 + 0.3x \times 8 + 0.1x \times 6}{x} = 0.6 \times 5 + 0.3 \times 8 + 0.1 \times 6 = 3 + 2.4 + 0.6 = 6.$$

Problem 5. Solution:
The area of the original rectangle is $A = WL$.
The area of the new rectangle is $A1 = (0.6W)(1.4L) = 0.84WL = 0.84A$.
So the area of the rectangle decreased by $1 - 0.84 = 0.16 = 16\%$.

Problem 6. Solution: (D).
After first year the weight will be $10 + 10 \times 11\% = 10\,(1.11)$
After second year the weight will be $10\,(1.11) + 10\,(1.11) \times 11\% = 10\,(1.11)(1.11) = 10\,(1.11)^2$.

After third year the weight will be $10\,(1.11)^2 + 10\,(1.11)^2 \times 11\% = 10\,(1.11)^2$ $(1.11) = 10\,(1.11)^3$.

Therefore after n years the weight will be $10\,(1.11)^n$.

Problem 7. Solution: 22.5.

$$\frac{9}{200} \times 500 = 22.5.$$

Problem 8. Solution: 40%.

$$\frac{x}{100} \times 500 = 200 \qquad \Rightarrow \qquad x = 40.$$

Problem 9. Solution: 256.

$$64 = \frac{25}{100} \times x \qquad \Rightarrow \qquad x = 256.$$

Problem 10. Solution: 400000.

$$6000 = \frac{3}{200} \times x \qquad \Rightarrow \qquad x = 400000.$$

Problem 11. Solution: 60.

Let x be the number of 9th graders and y be the number of 8th graders.

$$\frac{93x + 75y}{90} = 87 \text{ and } x + y = 90 \qquad \Rightarrow \qquad x = 60.$$

Problem 12. Solution: 60%.

$$\frac{10 + \dfrac{400}{900} \times 18}{12 + 18} = \frac{18}{30} = 0.6 = 60\%$$

Problem 13. Solution: $17.5.

Let x be the original price. $x \times \dfrac{60}{100} = 10.50 \qquad \Rightarrow \qquad x = 17.5.$

Problem 14. Solution: $56.

Let x be the price before the sale. $x \times \dfrac{65}{100} = 36.40$ $\Rightarrow$ $x = 56$.

Problem 15. Solution: 68%.

$d = d_1 + d_2 - d_1 d_2,$ $\Rightarrow$ $d = 20 + 15 - 3 = 32.$

$\therefore \; S = 250 - (0.32)(250) = (0.68)(250)$, That is, 68% of 250.

Problem 16. Solution: $15.

Let x be the original price.

The sale price after two discounts will be: $\dfrac{80}{100} \times \dfrac{75}{100} \times 25 = 15$

Problem 17. Solution: 42 percent.

The percent discounted: $\dfrac{30}{100} + \dfrac{40}{100} - \dfrac{30}{100} \times \dfrac{40}{100} = \dfrac{42}{100} = 58\%$.

The percent by which the original price been reduced: $1 - 58\% = 42\%$.

Problem 18. Solution: $ 10.

The interest paid for 12 months is $200 \times 0.12 = 24$. For 8 months it will be

$\dfrac{24}{12} \times 5 = 10$.

Problem 19. Solution: 74.

$\text{Average} = \dfrac{20 \cdot 80 + 30 \cdot 70}{20 + 30} = 74.$

Problem 20. Solution: $1000.

$12{,}000 = H - \dfrac{1}{5} H; \; \therefore H = 15{,}000, \quad 12{,}000 = S + \tfrac{1}{5}S; \; \therefore \; S = 10{,}000, \quad H + S =$

$25{,}000.$

Therefore, the sale resulted in a loss of $1000.

Problem 21. Solution: B.

Let C be the original price of the dress. Then $25 = C - 2.50$ or $C = 27.50$. $250/2750 = 1/11 \sim 9\%$.

Problem 22. Solution: 10 liters.

Name	C	V	S
A	0	x	0
B	0.9	8	7.2
Mixture	0.40	$8 + x$	$0.4(8 + x)$

$7.2 = 0.4(8 + x)$ $\Rightarrow$ $x = 10$ liters.

Problem 23. Solution: 30 liters.

Name	C	V	S
A	0	x	0
B	0.2	10	2
Mixture	0.05	$10 + x$	$0.05(10 + x)$

$2 = 0.05(10 + x)$ $\Rightarrow$ $x = 30$ liters.

Problem 24. Solution: 250 grams.

Name	C	V	S
A	0.05	x	$0.05x$
B	0.2	500	100
Mixture	0.15	$500 + x$	$0.15(500 + x)$

$0.05x + 100 = 0.15(500 + x)$ $\Rightarrow$ $x = 250$ grams.

Problem 25. Solution: (B). 20%.

	Name	C	V	S
Step 1	A	0.30	m	$0.3m$
	B	0	x	0
	Mixture	0.24	$x + m$	$0.24(x + m)$

146

Step 2	D	0.24	$x + m$	$0.24(x + m)$
	E	0	x	0
	Mixture	y	$x + m + x$	$y(2x + m)$

$0.3m = 0.24(x + m)$ $\Rightarrow$ $m = 4x$

$0.24(x + m) = y(2x + m)$ $\Rightarrow$ $0.24(x + 4x) = y(2x + 4x)$ $\Rightarrow$ $y = 0.2$
$= 20\%$.

Problem 26. Solution: (A). 19/20.

Name	C	V	S
A	0.855	100	85.5
B	0.9	x	$0.9\,x$

The substance does not change before or after the evaporation: $85.5 = 0.9x \Rightarrow x = 95$.

The answer is $95/100 = 19/20$.

Problem 27. Solution: (C).
There are $100 - 46 - 46 = 8$ percent of red staples. $4600 \times 0.08 = 368$ red staples.

Problem 28. Solution: 4000.
Let x be the amount of sales in that week.
We have $800 + 0.3x = 600 + 0.35x$ $\Rightarrow$ $0.05x = 200$ $\Rightarrow$ $x = 2000$.

Problem 29. Solution: 288.

$24 = \dfrac{25}{300} \times x$ $\Rightarrow$ $x = 288$.

Problem 30. Solution: 20.

$\dfrac{25}{200} \times 160 = 20$.

Problem 31. Solution:

We translate the sentence "what percent of $(q + r)$ is r" into the following math expression:

$$\frac{x}{100} \times (q + r) = r \qquad \Rightarrow \qquad x = \frac{100r}{q+r}.$$

So $\dfrac{100r}{q+r}$ percent of $(q + r)$ is r. Note that $\dfrac{100r}{q+r}$ percent is the same as $\dfrac{100r}{q+r}\%$.

Problem 32. Solution: D.
Since a single discount d, equal to three successive discounts d_1, d_2, and d_3, is $d = d_1 + d_2 + d_3 - d_1 d_2 - d_2 d_3 - d_3 d_1 + d_1 d_2 d_3$, then the choices are:
$$0.20 + 0.20 + 0.10 - 0.04 - 0.20 - 0.20 + 0.004 = 0.424 \text{ and}$$
$$0.40 + 0.05 + 0.05 - 0.02 - 0.02 - 0.0025 + 0.001 = 0.4585.$$
The saving is $0.0345 \times 10{,}000 = 345$(dollars).

Problem 33. Solution: (D).
The interest paid for 12 months is $750 \times 0.075 = 56.25$. For 8 months it will be
$$\frac{56.25}{12} \times 8 = 37.5.$$
Ann will owe $750 + 37.5 = \$787.50$.

Problem 34. Solution: (B).

Name	C	V	S
A	0	x	0
B	0.1	y	0.1y
Mixture	0.03	10	0.3

$$0.3 = 0.1y \qquad \Rightarrow \qquad y = 3 \text{ litres} \qquad \Rightarrow \qquad x = 10 - 3 = 7 \text{ litres.}$$

CPSIA information can be obtained
at www.ICGtesting.com
Printed in the USA
FSOW03n1207180517
34399FS